Sermons for Advent & Christmas

Sermons for

Advent &
Christmas

Selections from
Concordia Pulpit
Resources

CONCORDIA PUBLISHING HOUSE · SAINT LOUIS

MORE SELECTIONS FROM CONCORDIA PULPIT RESOURCES

Sermons for Funerals, Weddings & Civil Holidays (15-5103)

Sermons for Feasts, Festivals & Occasions (15-5104)

Sermons for Lent and Easter (15-5106)

Copyright © 2008 Concordia Publishing House
3558 S. Jefferson Ave., St. Louis, MO 63118-3968
1-800-325-3040 • www.cph.org

Unless otherwise noted, Scripture quotations are from The Holy Bible, English Standard Version®. Copyright © 2001 by Crossway Bibles, a publishing ministry of Good News Publishers, Wheaton, Illinois. Used by permission. All rights reserved.

Scripture quotations marked NIV are taken from the HOLY BIBLE, NEW INTERNATIONAL VERSION®. NIV®. Copyright © 1973, 1978, 1984 by International Bible Society. Used by permission of Zondervan Publishing House. All rights reserved.

Hymn texts with the abbreviation *LSB* are from *Lutheran Service Book*, copyright © 2006 Concordia Publishing House. All rights reserved.

Some material taken from *Lutheran Service Book: Altar Book*, copyright © 2006 Concordia Publishing House. All rights reserved.

The quotations marked AE are from Luther's Works, American Edition: vol. 21 copyright © 1956 by Concordia Publishing House. All rights reserved.

Manufactured in the United States of America

Library of Congress Cataloging-in-Publication Data

Sermons for Advent and Christmas : selections from Concordia pulpit resources.
     p. cm.
     ISBN 978-0-7586-1379-0
     1. Advent sermons. 2. Christmas sermons. I. Concordia pulpit resources. II. Title.

BV4254.5.S39 2008
252'.61—dc22

1 2 3 4 5 6 7 8 9 10   17 16 15 14 13 12 11 10 09 08

Contents

The Postures of Advent

Dr. Donald F. Hinchey

Advent 1

On Your Toes

Mark 13:33

Those of you who have belonged to a health club have, no doubt, met some very cruel women or men called aerobics instructors. They get paid to keep people like us in shape. We come limping to the workout floor, bone-tired after a hard day's work or barely awake from a night's sleep. They shout at us, "On your toes! Stretch! Move those muscles!" Then for an hour they run us through some of the most strenuous exercises imaginable.

Of course, aerobics instructors aren't cruel. They're merely helping us to get and keep in shape.

That's one of the functions of Advent as well. Here at the beginning of the Church Year we're reminded that while faith is a gift of God through Jesus Christ, it takes some work to keep that faith life vibrant and strong. It's simply too tempting to become an observer, not only during Advent but throughout the Church Year as well. During our Advent worship this year, we're going to assume various "faith postures." This week our Lord would shake us from being "Christian couch potatoes" with the command, "On your toes!"

THE COMMAND

"Be on guard, keep awake," our Lord tells us today. Over the centuries, some have considered Him cruel for these words. They took Him seriously, living as though Jesus were returning any moment, only to be disappointed when the months stretched into years and decades and there was no sign of His return. They prayed with Isaiah:

> Oh that You would rend the heavens and come down, that the mountains might quake at Your presence—as when fire kindles brushwood and the fire causes water to boil—to make Your name known to Your adversaries, and that the nations might tremble at Your presence! (Is 64:1–2)

But Jesus did not come. He only spoke again the command through Mark and the other evangelists: "Be on guard, keep awake! On your toes!" These words, like the words of the aerobics instructor, were not spoken in sadistic cruelty, but in love—for the good of the Church. Jesus speaks these words to us who tire so easily of waiting, who are so accustomed to instant gratification: "Be on guard, keep awake! On your toes!" Await the coming of the Lord like a child straining on tiptoes for a glimpse of the coveted Christmas gifts.

Jesus knew that the time of His coming is firmly established in the heart of His Father. When pressed for specifics, He repeatedly sidestepped the disciples' demands, finally and firmly telling them, "But concerning that day or that hour, no one knows, not even the angels in heaven, nor the Son, but only the Father" (Mark 13:32). And then our command: "Be on guard, keep awake" (v. 33). On your toes!

Our task as Christ's people is to be vigilant and expectant, trusting Jesus' words simply because He said them: "I will come again."

JESUS WILL COME

We know that Jesus will come again. He will come surely, certainly for each of us at the moment of our death. Who can tell the day or the hour? For some here tonight it may be a decade—perhaps, by God's grace, twenty or thirty years. For others, Judgment Day may be within the month or the week.

The second Epistle of Peter tells us, "But do not overlook this one fact, beloved, that with the Lord one day is as a thousand years, and a thousand years as one day" (2 Pet 3:8). A cartoon published a number of years ago has two shabbily dressed bums talking to God. "Is it true," says one to God, "that a minute in your time is as a thousand years?" "Yes," comes the voice from the cloud. "And is it true then," the shifty derelict continues, "that a penny is as a million dollars?" "Yes," the voice replies. The old bum says slyly, "Can I have a penny?" The voice from the cloud replies, "Just a minute."

We run into problems when we assume that God works in our time frame. Theologians have a word for it: anthropomorphizing, making God behave on human terms. We wrap up God in neat packages of our own expectations and then bemoan the fact that God won't perform as we think is proper.

Jesus knows better. It is not God's responsibility to live up to our expectations. It is our responsibility to live up to God's! We are on God's calendar; God is not on ours. We wait on God.

But this is not a passive activity—this waiting. This is not the helpless waiting of the victim awaiting attack. It is the expectant "on the toes" posture of the Olympic medalist who has run the race, finished in the lead, and now awaits the drop of the medal around his or her neck.

9

Two Dangers

God's people realize that there are dangers in prolonged waiting. Let me highlight two for you.

The first danger is that you can get lulled into a false sense of security as you wait. That false sense of security was a problem for Christians in St. Paul's day. The promise of their Lord to come was a lively hope for first generation Christians, but as this generation died, a second generation ran the risk of forgetting. That lively flame of hope that empowered the Church flickered and nearly was extinguished. "Behold! I tell you a mystery," Paul shouts to a drowsing Church. "We shall not all sleep, but we shall all be changed" (1 Cor 15:51).

The expectation of Jesus' coming is meant to stir us, shake us, hold us to the course of faith, and keep our eyes focused on the horizon for His coming. When we develop a false sense of security, the temptation becomes great to look to false gods for our blessings, and to forget the God of the cross, the One who out of love offered His Son into death for us. Lesser gods seem to be able to produce for us now! Why bother to wait for the coming Lord? To such a false sense of security, Jesus would command a posture change: "On your toes!" He says. "Be on guard, keep awake! Put away false gods and prepare to meet the crucified, resurrected, victorious Son of Man!"

The second danger of prolonged waiting is hopelessness. Those who grow weary of waiting for the Lord may soon grow weary of life itself. The roots of depression, mental health professionals tell us, are many. The psychiatrist may see a cause in a long-forgotten family pattern. A physician may look for some physical explanation. The psychologist notices certain patterns of unrealistic thinking. A pastor, however, often notices that the depressed, hopeless person is someone who, for whatever reason, is no longer waiting for God to intervene in life. Whatever the cause, depression pushes away from us the very thing we need the most—the sense of God's presence in our lives. When we cease to wait for God, we lose hope.

To the hopeless or the falsely secure, the command is the same: "On your toes!" Be active in your watching, your waiting! God is just around the corner. He offers signs of His coming everywhere if we simply train our eyes to see them. He will come, for our Lord promised, and He's not given to empty promises.

A God Who Keeps Promises

God says, "I will send Emmanuel," and, in the fullness of time, Mary and Joseph journey to Bethlehem and a promise is kept. There were plenty who slept through the incarnation, but those who were "on their toes" saw the promise being kept.

God says, "I will save!" In this Baby, through this Teacher, on a cross, that promise is kept. Our Lord Jesus whispered, "It is finished," on that crude wooden throne. "Finished" here means "fulfilled." What was finished was centuries of waiting for our salvation. On that cross is fulfilled all the longing that yearns in the hearts of God's people. The glory of the Lord was revealed in the death of His Son. The glory of the Lord was revealed as the dead body of Mary's Son becomes filled with God's life; and His resurrection and our resurrection become one. When God promises, it happens. Our waiting will be over.

Our Lord says, "This is My body . . . My blood; take, eat, . . . drink." Those who wait on their toes, eager to see the signs, see not merely the bread that crumbles in the hand and the wine in the cup. They know Christ's body and blood are there, given for the forgiveness of their sins. Others may shake their heads at what they consider such "naiveté," but the ones who are "on their toes" know that God keeps His promises.

LIVING ON YOUR TOES

Whether it is a manger, a cross, an open tomb, or bread and wine on the altar, the ones "on their toes" are always seeing signs of His coming. And they live with such watchfulness. Every day becomes a new joy. Every relationship becomes an opportunity to see Christ revealed in the other person. Every opportunity to serve and to care becomes an opportunity to look for Christ's coming in new and fresh ways! Do you sense the excitement of being "on your toes"? It's a call to live in expectation.

We so easily slip back into the routines of business as usual, that old pattern of expecting that all will be the same as it was last year and years before. You know it's happening when the church committee plans future activities by asking, "What did we do last year?" or when you say of yourself, "You can't teach an old dog new tricks." What we're saying is, "I really don't expect that God will come to me any differently than He has in the past."

The shadow of hopelessness can envelop us if we're not watching, not waiting expectantly, not on our toes. That's why God gives us signs like these we see in Advent in this place: one simple light on a wreath, to be joined by others on the way to a circle of fulfillment; one empty manger awaiting a King; bread and wine awaiting the words of our Lord; a congregation of fellow saints awaiting your love and fellowship; the whole Church on earth and countless hosts in heaven awaiting the final coming of our Lord in glory. And He will come. He said so. We stretch high on our toes. Come quickly, Lord Jesus! Amen.

Advent 2

On Your Knees

Mark 1:4

To one great Church father he was the "great forerunner of the morn." To the nineteenth-century sculptor Rodin he was "the precursor." Most of us know him as John the Baptist, but coming as he does in the midst of the world's Christmas season, he might well have earned the title "the killjoy." For this is the season of mirth and merriment, office parties and liquid cheer. We want to put aside gloom and doom, and it irks us to run into anything or anyone who will ruin our good Christmas time.

But every year, predictable as the credit card bills, comes John the Baptizer, cousin of Jesus, screaming his call for repentance. A wild sort of a man was he, whose idea of a gourmet meal was a handful of locusts and a glob of wild honey. He'd be out of place at one of our Christmas parties where everyone is decked out in velour and Brooks Brothers suits. John comes to our season with a one-piece camel hair original and a wide leather belt. And if his appearance and diet aren't bizarre enough, his message seems the ultimate killjoy. "Repent!" he cries. "On your knees! Change your mind and prepare the way of the Lord."

How out of sync with the world's view of Christmas. And yet, ironically, if the season is to mean anything to us, John must be heard!

John knows that you can't command people to be happy, and that is what our culture is doing to us at this time of year. It doesn't work. The philosopher Friedrich Nietzsche once observed that a party could always be found, but "the problem is finding enough people capable of enjoying one."

A trip to the local shopping mall reveals crowds of people with intense, grim expressions, crossing names off of penciled lists while calculating how much money remains before bankruptcy. Children cry because they can't get what they want when they want it. Alienated teens cynically slouch along the walls, feeling left out of the confusion, secretly wishing to belong. Clerks begin to show combat fatigue at this time of year, and the most harried, hassled man in the mall sits on a velour-covered chair in a red suit, trying to squeeze out a "Ho! Ho! Ho!" on cue.

The great irony, of course, is that while backs are being slapped and cheer is being drunk, lives are being lost as well. Christmas, we recall, is a prime time for suicides, as the command to be merry sounds for some like an unattainable demand. The sadness within people can be amplified by the season's expectation to be merry.

In fact, the meaning of the word *merry* in Old English was not "happy" as we know it today. Its original meaning was "peaceful." The old carol catches the sense of it: "God rest you merry, gentlemen." We often interpret that as if "merry" modified "gentlemen." But in fact it means "God rest you merry, gentlemen"—God grant peace to all gentlemen and gentlewomen through the Child of Christmas.

God comes to us at Christmas in a disarmingly simple and honest way. There is nothing more vulnerable than a baby, no one more needy than an infant. God presents Himself to us in utter honesty at Christmas. "All the world loves a baby," the cliché says. And in this most wonderful Child, all the world is loved *by* a baby. The infant in Bethlehem's barn satisfies our honest yearning for God.

The peace that comes this season comes in the form of a baby in a manger who enters this world to be our peace, who suffers and dies on a cross and then comes to life again. And what is the word with which He greets His followers? "Peace."

John the Baptizer is the forerunner of the Prince of Peace, and he knows that before we can experience the blessings of the season, we must first change our posture. We must take inventory and rid ourselves of those sinful barriers to the Prince's coming in our lives.

John won't let us off the hook: "Repent!" he cries in the wildernesses of our lives. Down on your knees is a good posture for that because it's hard to be haughty and arrogant when you're looking at someone else's kneecaps. As long as we're upright—walking about, doing "business as usual"—we can ignore the sin within. But on our knees we meet the sinful self, the self we've tried to ignore, which so troubles us and maintains a distance from God.

What we wait for at Advent is the forgiving grace of God in Jesus Christ. It was forged for us years ago on a cross outside of Jerusalem's city walls and was validated by angels at an empty tomb. We were submerged into that cleansing grace at our Baptism and clothed with the righteousness of Jesus Christ. But how hard it is to live in our Lord. How pervasive are the forces of sin and Satan that would woo us away from our baptismal identity as Christ's own.

John would have Israel and us confront that sinful self at the banks of the Jordan before we meet the Messiah in Bethlehem. We must come prepared for the encounter by repentance. The ancient Church knew that for years Advent was known as a "little Lent," a season of preparation for Christmas in the same way as Lent prepares us for Easter. Purple was the fitting hue of repentance in both seasons. The music had a sad and yearning quality about it, and there was pre-Christmas fasting in preparation for the infant Messiah. (Can you imagine that—fasting before Christmas?) We've pretty much given up that emphasis in our

Advent preparation. We just can't fight the culture that demands joy, even a super-ficial joy, at this time. But John won't let us forget.

"Repent," he demands of us. Let me suggest that Advent repentance is a three-step process: an Advent inventory, an Advent surrender, and an Advent acceptance.

We Take Inventory of Our Spiritual Decorations

Each year, somewhere around the second week of Advent, countless families descend or ascend to the storage parts of their houses to retrieve the boxes of Christmas decorations. There we find long-treasured ornaments, trinkets, and strings of lights that were hastily stuffed away last year, old pine needles still cling-ing to the clips. We dig into these boxes, often surprised by what treasures await us even if we've done this for a dozen or more years. This inventory of our Christmas decorations comes new to us each season.

That's the way it is with an Advent repentance inventory as well. We become so accustomed to living with our sins that we simply pack them away. We tend not to look at them or tend to deny them when others point them out to us.

But now at Advent, as we await our Lord's coming, John insists that we unpack and examine our individual sins: the pride that lifts me above others, insensitivity to the hurts around me, the jealousy and anger that have kept me apart from oth-ers and built a wall of resentment toward God. Decorating our lives with anger, jealousy, pride, and resentment in much the same way as we decorate our homes and Christmas trees might seem silly, but it is what we do. An Advent inventory helps us to take honest stock of ourselves and clean house.

We Surrender to a Gracious God

Next comes the hardest part. We surrender those painful, sinful aspects of our-selves to the God who can heal and restore, rescue and redeem. Don't you love to hear the Old Testament readings for the Advent season? They speak so confi-dently of our God as a restoring God. Listen:

> You, O Lord, are our Father, our Redeemer from of old is Your name. (Is 63:16)

> Behold, the Lord God comes with might, and His arm rules for Him; behold, His reward is with Him, and His recompense before Him. (Is 40:10)

> For as the earth brings forth its sprouts, and as a garden causes what is sown in it to sprout up, so the Lord God will cause righteousness and praise to sprout up before all the nations. (Is 61:11)

The God we meet at Christmas is a God who yearns to redeem people. Only those who repent receive this gracious gift of God. Those who feel they have no need for God's forgiveness ignore the message brought by the Child in the manger.

It's not that the act of repentance makes anyone acceptable to God. We are not saved because we repent. The prodigal son in Jesus' parable didn't even have time to mouth his carefully rehearsed repentance speech for his father. He was lifted up in the Father's waiting arms with the words still unspoken!

Rather, our repentance is an act of surrender to the God who would lift us up in love. God removes those heavy burdens of sin in order to lift us high in His gracious arms. At this time of year when the world is working so hard to be happy, the people of Christ surrender to God to be merry—to receive God's peace.

An Advent Acceptance

And the final response to John's cry for repentance is a holy intent to live the new life that is ours in Christ Jesus. Somewhere over the course of this holiday season you can bet we're going to hear on the television or radio the wish that the "spirit of Christmas" would extend beyond the season. It's a noble wish that we all share. And yet we seem to know better.

The good cheer that we experience fades as January's days approach. The old tensions of the workplace return, and for those in the northern hemisphere at least, the cold and gray reality of winter will soon make Christmas a memory.

It doesn't have to be this way for Christ's repentant people. The Messiah who comes to us at Advent will not go away. He will remain a constant, forgiving, restoring presence in our lives. What remains for us is to remember who we are:

We are the forgiven ones. Let's forgive! We are God's loved ones in Christ. Let's love! We are those visited by God. Let's visit others with God's love!

To repent of our sins and surrender ourselves to our redeeming God now means living in the reality of that forgiveness. God has rested us merry, gentlewomen and men. Let's live in that peace!

A flippant bumper sticker in a gift shop read, "Repent!" and then in smaller letters, "If you have already repented, please disregard this notice."

In fact, we are forever repenting; forever taking inventory and surrendering; forever returning to the amazing grace of God in Christ Jesus. Let us assume an Advent posture of repentance this year. The only way to be close to the Child in the manger is on our knees. He will reach His tiny hand out from the straw and touch us with His love.

Advent 3

With Eyes Wide Open

Luke 1:8–23, 57–63

Advent is not a season for the stagnant and sedentary. We've been talking about the postures of Advent over the past weeks, and what I've suggested is that this time of the year is a time for action. There's enough pointless busyness at this time of the year. Any trip to the shopping mall will tell us that!

But the action that Advent requires is of a different sort. It's a yearning for God, an anxious waiting for His coming. We called that "on your toes." It's time for repentance, for turning back to God. "On your knees," John the Baptizer called last week. And tonight we hear a call to look for signs of God's coming all around us. We approach Christmas "with eyes wide open."

When we stop to think about it, this time of the year can become a closed-in time. We can become locked in by responsibilities and routine. Physically, when the weather turns cold and forbidding, people shut themselves into their homes. Into this kind of closed-off world comes Advent, an invitation to open up.

You'll hear it in our Scripture lessons each week. God appears to people who have their futures all decided and locked up, and He tells them that there will be some changes and they'd best get ready!

To the carpenter Joseph—open up! You will be a father but not by your own action. To the teenage Mary and her elderly cousin Elizabeth—open up! God is entering your lives in a miraculous way. You are each going to have a child. Neither of you thought that this would happen, but it is by the grace of God, and the world will not be the same. And tonight a call to openness comes to Elizabeth's husband, Zechariah, and to us as well.

Open your eyes! See what is right in front of you, and let your faith in God inform your vision. Zechariah has an encounter with the angel Gabriel, and for his spiritual blindness, he is struck dumb. It's a strange punishment, isn't it? Why not blindness for blindness? That would seem appropriate.

But Zechariah is a priest, and one of the most important tasks of a priest is blessing people. After offering incense, he would exit the holy place, raise his arms, and pronounce the benediction: "The Lord bless you and keep you . . ."

But if you're struck dumb, you can't do that! A blessing should not be given by one who doubts God, but only by those who believe His Word. After following the angel's command to name the child as God said, Zechariah's tongue is set loose. "His name shall be John," he says, and he speaks to everyone's amazement.

Advent announces that God is coming into our midst, but we struggle to see signs of God's presence. Why is it that we cannot see God when He comes to us? Why are our eyes so closed to God's coming?

Maybe it's just that it seems too good to be true. You sense that when Mary encounters the angel Gabriel. After she has gotten over the fright of being visited by a celestial warrior, she gasps, "Who, me? You can't be serious! Why me, when there are so many other girls around? What makes me so privileged?"

We are so used to bad news that when the good news comes, we stand back as if we are evaluating a salesman's offer that is too good to be true. If it were you or I standing in front of that altar with Zechariah today, we probably would do the same thing, wouldn't we? "How shall I know this?" Zechariah says about Elizabeth's pregnancy. "For I am an old man, and my wife is advanced in years" (v. 18).

How shall we know that God comes to us? The world continually trembles on the brink of war and no one's job is safe. Friends become ill and die. Children suffer, marriages dissolve, and we are exposed to all kinds of evil day after day. Where is God?

I would like to believe with my whole heart the message of the angel by the altar, but my heart cannot. The doubt within me is constant and nagging. If Gabriel appeared beside our altar today, we might call for five of our biggest ushers to try to throw him out the door! What he has to say is simply too good to be true!

Why can't we see? Perhaps because we're afraid of what might become of us if we do see. When we acknowledge things, we know we have to acknowledge their consequences as well.

Physicians have seen it time and time again. A patient has been suffering with some ailment for an incredibly long period of time, but they've ignored it and pretended it isn't there: a lump in the breast, a sore throat, or a pain in the gut. By the time it can no longer be ignored, it is too late to cure. "Why didn't you come in earlier?" the doctor asks in frustration. "Because I was afraid of what it might be," the patient answers.

Couples will ignore pain in their relationship for years before seeking marital therapy or talking with their pastor. And by the time they meet with the pastor, often the marriage is almost over. "Why didn't you come in when this started?" the pastor asks. "We didn't want to bother you. We didn't have the money for the counselor or the time." But the real reason is fear that some changes will have to be made for the bad news to get better.

When God comes to us to claim us, to take control of our lives, somehow life will be different after the encounter. Perhaps it will be more risky, as God calls us

17

to live on the edge by faith. Zechariah's life could not be the same when he became the aged father of the forerunner of the Messiah. Mary could not live as though she were not the mother of the Son of God. And when God comes to us, our lives are not the same either.

It's kind of scary when you stop to think about it. Wonderfully scary! But God comes anyway to us, and especially so at Advent. God comes and beckons us to open our eyes to His coming.

Babies are seemingly innocent and precious. If they're not yours, they don't demand much. A baby would be a very comfortable symbol for God's coming to us—cute to look at, soft to touch, and for the most part controllable, manageable, and safe.

Yet on another level, it's absolutely scandalous. God, whom we assume is going to flex divine muscle and set the nations straight, humbles Himself to come into our midst in the most vulnerable way. That might mean God rules and would have us rule not through power but through love, innocence, and self-sacrifice. Wars and arguments were never won that way! If our eyes are opened this Advent to see the baby in the manger as God in weak human flesh, we must reevaluate how we flex our muscles as we demand and claw for power.

And what of the baby grown? What of Jesus the teacher? What of His demanding, confrontational teachings? What of His healings?

And what of Jesus the crucified? What of His cross? That's at least as big a scandal as the manger, isn't it? To see God on the cross moves us to a faith that is absolutely life-changing. To know that He suffered that cross for you and me means that we can never live for ourselves again. We need never pummel ourselves with past sins, since they were nailed with Jesus to His cross. They have been put to death with death. We are forgiven, and we need never use the past as a barrier to keep us from facing the future with Him. With eyes wide open, we see ourselves for who we are: forgiven sons and daughters of God. We are free to live for this amazing God, if we, with eyes wide open, see Him for who He is.

Advent is a time for clarified vision. It is a time to live with eyes wide open! It is an invitation to stand before the altar with Zechariah the priest, and for these weeks to shut our mouth and open our eyes.

It is a truism in counseling that the way to be of assistance to troubled people is through silent listening. Counselors are instructed to close their mouths, open their eyes and ears, and be attentive to the person in front of them. You can't really see what is in front of you with your mouth open!

That's good advice for this Advent season as well. One of our favorite hymns at this time of year is "O Little Town of Bethlehem," and one of the most beautiful verses of that hymn sings:

How silently, how silently
The wondrous gift is giv'n!
So God imparts to human hearts
The blessings of His heav'n.
No ear may hear His coming;
But in this world of sin,
Where meek souls will receive Him, still
The dear Christ enters in. (*LSB* 361:3)

May we train our eyes to see God in this holy season—to see Him in silence in the midst of the noise, to see His light in the darkness. He's here. He's on the altar in the bread and wine. In His Holy Scriptures, He is waiting to talk to you. He is in the brother, sister, and child next to you in the pew. The signs are everywhere, if we but open our eyes.

The dear Christ enters into our world this year, as He has entered every year. He came to us in Holy Baptism. He is active in our lives. The only question is, Will we see Him? Will our eyes be opened to His presence?

Advent Series Based on Hymns

Rev. Richard W. Patt

Advent 1

The Season before the Season

Matthew 25:1–13

"Wake, Awake, for Night Is Flying" (*LSB* 516)

A few years ago, right after Thanksgiving, I received a letter sent out by a friend. It was his annual Christmas greeting, sent to a host of friends. Toward the end of his beautifully composed thoughts, he spoke about the days of Advent ahead. Almost as a warning, it seemed, he wrote, "Observe them carefully."

I have never forgotten his words. When the days of Advent roll around every year, I remember my friend's appeal. "Observe them carefully." Advent, you see, is the season before the season. There's no question that the season coming is Christmas. Emotionally, it's the biggest celebration we engage in as Christians—even though our theology and liturgy point to Easter as the supreme festival. Then, too, Christmas is the celebration that can make or break us economically, whether as customers or merchants. It's simply the biggest day around for almost everyone. We put a lot of stock in Christmas!

Because of this, it's good advice to observe carefully the days that lead up to Christmas. It would be a shame to prepare poorly—or lightly—for this great festival. More sadly, it would be a total shame if we missed the whole point of Christmas, hence my friend's warning, "Observe them carefully!" And thus we have this "season before the season." Advent is the time to observe carefully the great season of Christmas!

Today *(tonight)*, one of those jubilant Advent hymns of the Church will help us and guide us.

The hymn "Wake, Awake, for Night Is Flying" was written by a German Lutheran pastor, Philipp Nicolai, who lived shortly after Martin Luther. It is based on our text, Mt 25:1–13, and other Scripture references. The English translation comes to us from a great translator, Catherine Winkworth. Pastor Nicolai was considered a genius, not only for his beautiful poetry and great preaching but also for his talent as a composer. Some Lutherans consider this tune to be the king of chorales, and the tune he composed for "O Morning Star, How Fair and Bright" (*LSB* 395) to be the queen of chorales.

"Wake, Awake, for Night Is Flying" leads us down two main tracks of thought. The first stanza of the hymn starts us down the first track. Let's sing *(or read)* the first stanza now. *(Sing or read the first stanza.)*

In these words, Philipp Nicolai introduces us to an Advent parable that Jesus once told, the parable of the sleeping maidens. *(Read parable.)* Like the Christmas letter from my friend, the message of this charming parable and the hymn is a warning. Wake, awake! Observe carefully these days before Christmas. Watch what you are doing. Be aware of what is happening.

For all the gravity of this message, the parable relates a rather lighthearted occasion, almost a game. In Jesus' day, you see, people liked to inject into the wedding scene some playful, surprising elements, similar to our practice of throwing rice over the newlyweds or tying a clump of empty tin cans to the rear bumper of the honeymoon car.

One of these surprising elements included the bridegroom's arrival at the bride's home before the wedding ceremony in order to claim her and her attendants. At this point he would take them—and the families and wedding guests—to the wedding hall for the ceremony, the reception, and the honeymoon. These events together could last seven days or more! The playful part of it all was the challenge to the bridegroom to arrive at the bride's home at a moment that would catch her and her maidens unprepared. What better time to pull off such a surprise than some hour during the middle of the night? That's the scene the song describes. *(Read stanza one.)*

Christmas is coming soon, and this "season before the season" bids us to watch, wake, be ready, prepare, and observe these days carefully. What is it that we are to be so careful about during this season before the season?

Let me put it this way (and you will have to follow this thought closely). During this season of Advent, we are to become aware that the coming season, Christmas, is never complete in itself. The Christmas season only has a fully productive meaning for us as we sense and experience its fulfillment during the seasons of Lent and Easter. To put it in visual terms, Advent calls us to see the cross of Jesus hovering over the manger. The joy of the Christmas season comes to its fullness after repentance over our sins and trust in the forgiveness of the cross and the victory of the open tomb. As we gaze into the quiet skies of a Christmas silent night, we need to discern a triumphant, risen Savior coming toward us in Last Day victory.

You see, the second track of thought the hymn writer leads us down is a vision of the resplendent, overflowing joy that comes as we receive the Christ of Judgment Day and enter into the heavenly home. In a few moments I'm going to invite you to sing about that joy in the last two stanzas of the hymn. But right now, this season of Advent calls us to discern very carefully and precisely what it is about the coming season of Christmas that can bring us to such unbounded and genuine inner joy, as these words of the hymn describe it for us so lavishly.

This is all another way of asking, "What really is the Gospel of Christmas?" For some, a kind of gospel during the coming weeks will be the Christmas spirit charmingly presented in irresistible characters such as the Grinch, Scrooge, the Little Match Girl, or, in ultimate fashion, Santa Claus himself. Or, as this age becomes increasingly one in which we create unrealistic images of life, the gospel of the season may come in the form of family tradition. Magazines and craft shows and recipe books show us how to create illusions of softness and the glow of yesteryear in our homes. These shimmering holiday images become a kind of gospel that covers over serious family tensions and dysfunction. After Christmas, sad to say, this false gospel leaves us as soon as we take down all the decorations. Then we are left in the glare of the same troubled relationships that burdened us before.

For still others, the gospel of the coming season will arrive in the form of "baby Jesus." Parents will openly talk about Him. Even distinguished entertainers will touchingly share with us the songs and poetry about this little stranger. It is as though during an encounter with baby Jesus we will be magically transformed. Somehow cold hearts will be melted. The hard side of our behavior will be softened in response to the appeal, "Come on, it's Christmas!"

These gospels are all difficult to reject precisely because they feel so right. But the warning of Advent comes to say, "Keep watch, awake!" The profound joy that the hymn writer here speaks of springs from a richer and fuller Gospel than Christmas spirit or family tradition or isolated scenes involving baby Jesus; a Gospel that also devastates the other quaint, sentimental Christmas "gospels." This is a Gospel about the King of kings and Lord of lords. Advent bids us meet the awesome Son of God, who came from the Father in the mystery of virgin birth—Christ Jesus among us in the degradation of a drafty manger; the poor one, pressed to flee the land in tender infancy; the Savior of the world, crucified, died, buried, and risen again, seated at the Father's right hand until He comes again in glory. This Christ of the Nativity and Lent and Easter brings a joy so full and embracing that the halls of heaven echo with jubilation. This is the full Christmas Gospel!

This season before the season warns us not to miss any of that! Do not miss the joy that reaches deep—this joy of salvation that changes everything: history, hearts, and homes. Do not miss the Gospel that makes us new people! For it is the cross of Christ that forgives our sin; His blood cleanses our hearts. Raised with Him by the power of the Spirit, we are overtaken by a living Easter faith that instills in us a joyful determination to live as the people of God.

Can we sing of this joy that comes our way in Jesus Christ, as the hymn writer penned it? Yes! We can sing it! Wide awake, let us now set our joy to music as we sing! *(Sing stanzas two and three.)*

Advent 2

The Uncomfortable Work of Comforting

Isaiah 40:1–5

"Comfort, Comfort Ye My People" (*LSB* 347)

There are usually two sides to everything. That includes the Gospel we proclaim in the Church. One "side" of the Gospel has to do with something very comforting. God speaks tenderly to each one of us. He doesn't shout at us. What He whispers in our ear is welcome news indeed: "Your hard service has been completed; your sin has been paid for." For any sinner that's a comforting word—wouldn't you agree?

But then there is the other side of the Gospel. It's the side that reminds us of the great cost the Father required from His Son in payment for our sins. It's the side that warns us against "cheap grace." It also reminds us that as we readily accept God's comforting Word, we hear a call to bring others this same comfort and encouragement.

The "other side" of the Gospel acquaints us with the untidy, uncomfortable aspect of the Christian enterprise. It is sort of like what happened at our church several years ago when we began constructing the new addition. First, the builders cut off the convenient entrance from our main parking lot. That meant everyone had to take a long walk around the other side of our building in order to enter the church. The construction also created a mess. People tracked in mud and dirt. It was impossible to keep the sidewalks clean. And the noise! Our staff workers here at church sometimes went home feeling tense after listening to an air hammer or a bulldozer all day outside their window. Construction can often be an uncomfortable enterprise. Of course, now that the work is over and we are enjoying the brand-new facilities, we've forgotten the discomfort, and we relish the comfort of it all!

Sometimes we miss this challenging aspect behind the famous Advent prophecy here in Isaiah 40: "In the wilderness prepare the way of the LORD; make straight in the desert a highway for our God. Every valley shall be lifted up, and every mountain and hill be made low; the uneven ground shall become level, and the rough places a plain" (vv. 3–4). In between the poetic lines did you hear the air hammers and bulldozers? Did you cough in the dusty air or notice your newly polished shoes stuck in the mud? Bringing comfort has its uncomfortable side. Are we up to the challenge this Advent season?

The Advent hymn before us today *(tonight)* presents us with the spiritual discomfort involved in receiving the Advent message of comfort. The hymn "Comfort, Comfort Ye My People" is the work of a German court preacher and chaplain to a duke, Johann Olearius (1611–84). He originally wrote this hymn for the Festival of St. John the Baptist and based it on our text. In the third stanza of the hymn, the writer speaks about Advent "calling sinners to repentance." In the same stanza the writer lifts his finger: "O that warning cry obey!"

Together with Isaiah's picture of dismantling and uprooting and leveling, these phrases of the hymn present us with an essentially discomforting task. Despairing of our own power, our own spiritual contrivances, our own cleverly conceived plans about saving ourselves—with empty hands and an empty heart, we humbly wait for the true word of comfort God whispers to us: "Hard service has been completed. Your sin has been paid for." Yes, there's something that puts us all in an uncomfortable position when we have to admit that we human beings are weak— even powerless. We need a healing and mending within that we ourselves can never provide. It's tough to admit, "I can't do it myself." Few things in life make us prideful human beings feel more uncomfortable.

Advent sweeps away all our pride. Although it may make us uncomfortable, God says to us, "Your days of trying to gain My favor by being hard on yourself are over. Your sins are paid for—not by you, but by a Savior: My Son. Although you are still struggling with your sins and falling into temptation, He steadily walked to the cross and paid the price—the full cost—for your sinning ways. Through His agonizing crucifixion and death, your sins are paid for."

In Holy Baptism, we die to sin with Christ, then rise with Him to new life. Do you see the remodeling job Jesus has done on each of us? Paul the apostle says that God has made each of us in Christ "a new creation" (2 Cor 5:17). This amazing salvation message of Advent—and of Christmas and of Lent and of Easter—moves you and me into the spiritual comfort zone. What comfort indeed!

Because of this salvation message, we are pressed to move on and speak about the uncomfortable work of comforting others. The other side of the message is implicit in our text and the hymn, but it becomes explicit during the emerging Christmas season. The heart of this side of the message goes something like this: we have received this amazing comfort of the Gospel. Now you and I are called to bring comfort to those around us! No receiving comfort without giving comfort to others in response. It's another way of saying that love generates love; faith yields fruit; and the Christmas Gospel leads to "the Christmas spirit"—sharing and caring for others.

The coming Christmas season with its warmth and love is a paradigm of the way in which the people of God are to go about bringing comfort—day in and day out—to the broken, the poor, the needy, the dying, the ill, and all who suffer from injustice and the injurious pride of others. Advent prophets like Isaiah call us constantly to be engaged in the activity of comforting through human care.

In other places Isaiah sings about the eyes of the blind being opened and the ears of the deaf being unstopped. He talks about the poor and thirsty and needy being satisfied. He is talking about a Savior who does such things and about those people of the Savior who do likewise. He is talking about our common activity of bringing comfort to one another.

Now, bringing comfort can be—and usually is—hard work. That's the other side of the Gospel. Comforting others can be uncomfortable for us who are called to do it! It's similar to being inconvenienced for a while when the construction crew tore up the landscape around us.

The scenarios in the Christian community develop something like this: A woman is quite sick. She is in the hospital. She needs the kind of comfort we are talking about. She would be happy if any of our church members were to visit her. But potential comforters beg off, saying, "I feel uncomfortable around sick people; I never know what to say."

Another scenario involves the elderly—perhaps an old man in a nursing home is lonely much of the time. But potential visitors beg off, saying, "I feel uncomfortable around old people; besides, nursing homes make me feel depressed."

Then there is the troubled soul, known to many in the congregation, facing marriage and family problems. Just a little word of encouragement from any one of you could make such a difference. But potential encouragers beg off, saying, "I couldn't possibly do that! You see, I have an unwritten rule about never getting involved in other people's problems."

Or how about the teen who has just moved in across the street with her family? Teens in the congregation could do a lot by inviting someone like that to church or the youth group. But most of them beg off, saying, "If I'd do something like that, my friends—and probably the newcomer too—would think I was some kind of religious nut. That would make me feel uncomfortable!"

I suppose it would. But sometimes—maybe most of the time—that's the "other side" of the Gospel. Bringing comfort to hurting, broken people is rarely comfortable—or convenient, or something done quickly or easily. But it is that other side of the Gospel—our response to the comforting news of salvation in the cross of Jesus Christ. It is particularly the call during this Advent season. Do the uncomfortable work of comforting, and you will become a partner with Christ Himself as He carries out His ministry of love in the world today.

Advent 3

From the General to the Specific

Luke 3:1–15

"On Jordan's Bank the Baptist's Cry" (*LSB* 344)

One of our greatest failures is keeping things general when we ought to be getting specific. How much of a sense of love do we withhold because our love is general instead of specific? How many needy people remain so because our sympathy never quite moves us into action? How many persons have never learned about the love of Jesus Christ because, instead of talking about that, we have limited our conversations to religion in general?

The hymn "On Jordan's Bank the Baptist's Cry" was written in Latin by a Frenchman, a professor at the University of Paris, and first published in 1736. It was translated into English a hundred years later by a priest of the Church of England.

During this third week of Advent, both the Bible text before us and the hymn of the week we have chosen present us with a preacher who got quite specific with people about the things godly persons ought to be doing. That preacher, of course, was John the Baptizer. John was needed in his day in the same way that we need precise, clear preaching today concerning our call to bring care and healing to a broken world.

The Bible story before us is impressive in this connection. People were brought out of a mindset in which they seemed to be able to think only in generalities. The people here were so moved by John's preaching that they began asking specific questions, such as, "What then shall we do?" (v. 10). John answered their questions by pointing out definite ways in which they should change their behavior—ways that would also bring care and help to others.

John told them, for instance, that if they had two coats, they should give one to a person who had none. If they were blessed with more than enough to eat and drink, they should share the surplus with people who were going hungry. People in business were told specifically by John that they shouldn't overcharge or cheat a customer. People must stop being so money-hungry that they devise shady ways of obtaining it, like fudging the books, cheating on taxes, lying about a product, or twisting someone's arm. What's marvelous here is that John's Advent message moved these people to the point that they wanted to know very specifically what their response to God's call ought to be.

That is the way it always is with anything connected to the Gospel. The Gospel itself is very specific, isn't it? The message of God's love for us is not bandied about in gushy generalities. It is not just a bunch of words that sound religious or sacred. The Gospel is the Word of the Father, which took on specific form and flesh in the person of His Son, Jesus Christ, and the Spirit's work in reminding us of that Word. We do not have a disembodied or absentee Savior, but rather, as St. John put it, a Savior who "became flesh and dwelt among us" (Jn 1:14).

This Savior's life was the most specific ministry this world has ever seen. We could make endless lists of Jesus' definite acts of personal concern and deliverance. Jesus proclaimed God's love for the whole world—and that means each individual. In the ministry of Jesus we see that God's love always is very specific. Jesus heals specific people in specific ways. He forgives a woman of the night. He sits down at the table of a tax collector and they eat a meal together. A widow's son is raised from the dead. He puts mud on the eyes of a blind man, who then sees. A demon who torments a young man with self-destructive behavior is cast out at Jesus' command. One-on-one, Jesus applies His healing power.

Jesus continued the Father's work of rescue in a specific way. "He suffered under Pontius Pilate." On a hill named Golgotha, Pilate's soldiers erected a cross. Jesus allowed His own hands and feet to be nailed to it. For eternity they still bear the scars. On the third day there was something much more concrete than general talk about faith in the future or love conquering all. We weren't left with a vague rumor about how the memory of Jesus would keep Him alive, or how the spirit of His deeds would live on in the hearts of those who knew Him. No, the angel that spoke on that resurrection morn had a specific message of fact: "He has risen; He is not here. See the place where they laid Him" (Mk 16:6). Later, they saw Him with their own eyes.

Advent is the time to be catapulted out of the cocoon of religious generalities. It's a time to get real about our salvation and about our calling in response to it. John the Baptizer did that for his generation. He stood on the banks of the Jordan

River, and he preached. The people heard him. They responded. They wanted to know specifically how they should change their lives in response to God's impending salvation. They wanted to know how people of the kingdom should act and what they should do. They moved from the general to the specific.

Several years ago, the Roman Catholic archbishop in Central America, Oscar Romero, was slain. Among his memorable statements is this one: "Some want to keep the Gospel disembodied that it doesn't get us involved at all in the world it must save."[1] Such is often our problem: we keep our love so "disembodied" that it usually amounts to little more than a bunch of words. We like to keep the Gospel general, when in reality it speaks to each person quite pointedly.

God knows the value of being specific, of putting words into concrete form. God Himself took on the body of that baby in Bethlehem's manger. And as the Word made flesh, in whom the fullness of the Deity dwelt bodily, Jesus was always quite specific in how He demonstrated His universal love.

Talking about our hesitancy to get specific in serving God, author Elizabeth O'Connor put it this way: "I would much rather be committed to God in the abstract than be committed to him at the point of my gifts."[2] That is exactly where a lot of us might find ourselves in the midst of this blessed Advent season. We're being swept away by a lot of the spiritual generalities of the season, basking in the glow of Christmas. We have no particular idea what we're going to do with the gifts and talents God has given us—no specific plans to witness to the Gospel by caring for those who need care.

In fact, when asked to contribute our gifts, most of us usually respond by replying, "What gifts?" We have no clear idea which specific gifts God has given us because we have not tried very hard to exercise them in God's service. When you are interviewed for a job these days, you had better know exactly what job skills you possess and have experience in using, or the interviewer will walk away unimpressed. Advent is the time of God's job call to all Christians. The people responded to John by asking, "What then shall we do?" (Lk 3:10). Maybe our first question ought to be, "What specifically can I do to serve God in the spot God has placed me?"

As we purchase gifts for others, we also need to spend some of our Advent days searching out and detailing the gifts God has given us. Then we can write Him a thank-You note by using them in His service. For instance, do you have the gift of hospitality—the ability to extend a warm welcome to a stranger? Then use that gift to pay a visit to a newcomer in our church. Do you make or bake things

---

1 Marie Dennis, Renny Golden, and Scott Wright, *Oscar Romero: Reflections on His Life and Writings* (Maryknoll, NY: Orbis, 2000).

2 Elizabeth O'Connor, *Eighth Day of Creation* (Waco: Word, 1971).

with your hands? A sick, injured, or homebound member of the parish would feel encouraged and specially loved if you could share a craft item or a plate of your cookies with them. Has the Gospel of the Christ Child touched your heart? Why not speak heart-to-heart with someone who does not know the Savior? The Gospel needs to be embodied, even as God's love came to earth in an infant boy at Christmas. No more generalities, please, but a dynamic expression of the Gospel that Christ lived out among us—all the way to cross and resurrection. As we sing now about John the Baptizer, keep asking the question, "What then shall I do?" *(Sing the hymn.)*

Advent 4

His Exquisite Birth

Luke 1:31–33

"Savior of the Nations, Come" (*LSB* 332)

The innocent young couple Mary and Joseph; the hard but poignant journey from Nazareth to Bethlehem; the dank setting in a cattle shed; the crude animals surrounding the newborn Child; a huge, glistening star in the night sky; shepherds, awed by the sight of an angel; the melody of a thousand angels—all these components of the Christmas story add up to what we might call "His exquisite birth."

The Advent hymn we focus on in this service, originally written in Latin, dates back to St. Ambrose in the fourth century. Luther gave us a German version, and several different translators gave us our present English translation.

"Marvel now, O heav'n and earth, That the Lord chose such a birth" (*LSB* 332:1). The hymn is right. There are a host of exquisite features here that move us to talk about "His exquisite birth."

Of course, every birth of a child is wondrous in its way. Just about every adult has had the pleasure of holding a newborn in his or her arms. What an added sense of awe we feel when that is our own child, born of our flesh and blood.

We rightly speak about "the miracle of birth": tiny hands and fingernails; lips and eyes of lovely form; miniature arms and legs gently flexing themselves—who can resist these inspiring features? We affirm God's sacred gift of life in the womb and life freshly come from the womb. As a current slogan puts it, "It's not a choice, it's a child!" Life matters. Life counts. Life is so exquisite.

During Christmas we extend this honor beyond the human. We include animals (as does the Christmas story) as part of God's creation to be received with thanksgiving. Why do pictures of "all creatures great and small" often pop up on the covers of many of our Christmas cards? What is the source of the fanciful legends about "friendly beasts" we often hear during Christmas? Aren't these attempts to say that in some way all life (and all of God's creation) is sacred, and we are to honor it?

Birth and life are exquisite. Maybe that's why we feel especially shaken by a terrible phenomenon increasing in most of our urban areas these days: the untimely death of babies and small children because of so-called "drive-by shootings" or parental abuse or neglect. When we hear about such atrocities, we in the community of faith must do more than wring our hands or feel sorry. We must hear again the word of Jesus about becoming peacemakers. In an active way we have to offer children a more life-affirming reason to live than the reasons the gangs offer. Life is wondrously sacred, and we need to instill this value in children in vital ways that make a difference for them.

But when we talk about the Child born of Mary, the Bible text before us reminds us that despite the humble, earthy scene, there is a singular feature essential to "His exquisite birth": Jesus was born of a virgin mother. "The Holy Spirit will come upon you, and the power of the Most High will overshadow you" is the way the angel Gabriel explained it to Mary (Lk 1:35).

Here we come upon the supremely exquisite quality of the infant Jesus. It is the Holy Spirit of God who empowered the conception of this child.

What does this fact mean for us? What is so exquisite about this feature in the story of Jesus' birth? According to the angel (Lk 1:35), the conception of Jesus by the Holy Spirit is a sign of His divinity. The virgin birth is the indisputable fact that shows Jesus is the Son of God.

Jesus is the eternal Son of God—He always has been and always will be. In the Nicene Creed we affirm that He was "begotten, not made, being of one substance with the Father." This means that the virgin conception of Jesus did not "make" Him the Son of God, as if He were not so before. What, then, happened at His miraculous conception? St. John summarizes the Gospel story of Christmas by saying "the Word became flesh" (1:14). The eternal Word of God, who is forever the Son of God, came to us in human flesh as the Babe of Bethlehem. The Word became incarnate—Latin for "in flesh."

Did not, in fact, this virgin conception—this exquisite birth—serve as a marvelous signal for all time that God was acting in a unique way in the coming of Jesus? Look at this virgin-conceived child! He is the only one the world will ever see. Behold the virgin-born Son of God—yes! For in His coming, and in all of His life upon earth that follows, God was moving into action in an ultimate way to bring His rescuing and saving power to us creatures of flesh. God became one of us (but without sin) in order to redeem each of us.

Jesus' exquisite birth pushes us onward to behold His exquisite ministry as well, and then to behold His most exquisite death and resurrection. This Jesus comes as Savior, and in His coming God is acting with finality to save us from our sins.

Today, as we approach the culmination of the blessed Advent season, you and I must catch the profound significance of the exquisite signal God displayed for all humanity. As we review the biblical teaching about the virgin conception, it proclaims that the Son of God has come as the Father's final Word of love to you and me. In the virgin birth, cross, and resurrection of Jesus, God's love for you and me is expressed fully and completely; God's plan of salvation is fulfilled. God requires nothing more. And mankind, including ourselves, can contribute nothing to God's exquisite gift.

That is good news; it is exquisite news! It is news that we need to thrust outward until all people know of it and believe it. You and I must move beyond simply observing God's signal to the point where we are dynamically witnessing about it. That is part of the Advent call. Christ the exquisite-born is "Savior of the nations." In the hymn we pray that this Savior of the nations comes to each of us. But we are also challenged in this season to see to it that the message of His love and deliverance comes to people everywhere—to the nations.

In her pre-Christmas song, the Magnificat, Mary sang about a similar vision. "All generations will call me blessed" (Lk 1:48), she intoned. The Savior's virgin conception in her womb was an exquisite event because it was the Savior so conceived. "All generations" and "all nations" need to know of the salvation finally wrought by this Child as He died upon the cross and rose from the dead on Easter Day.

Last Christmas, the Associated Press released a story about the celebration of Christmas in Bethlehem, in the Holy Land. The story included an observation by a visiting tourist from Chicago, Todd Johnson, an insurance agent. Johnson reflected that it was a "great feeling" to be in Bethlehem, and he was excited to tell his friends that he had celebrated Christmas in the city of Jesus' birth. Soon you and I will celebrate too. We will go to Bethlehem here at our own altar. After hearing the good news of the Savior's exquisite birth, I hope we'll exclaim, too, "I can't wait until all my friends hear about it."

To encourage all in that task, let us now sing about this exquisite birth and about this Savior of the nations in our Advent hymn of the week. *(Sing the hymn.)*

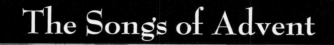

The Songs of Advent

Rev. Luther C. Brunette

Zechariah's Song: Amazing Gift

Luke 1:67–79

During these days leading up to Christmas, our world is bombarded with music, perhaps more than at any other time of the year. Surprisingly, much of the music is about our coming Savior, Jesus Christ. This is the only time of the year when we have the license to carry the message of Christ to a secular, pluralistic world.

A person can go into a shopping mall and hear even nonbelievers singing, "Christ, the Savior, is born." Go into grocery stores, offices, restaurants, and even taverns, and you may hear music about the Christ Child. Even the hard rock radio stations play Christmas music. Many public schools allow music about Jesus Christ to be sung by their choirs. This is the only time of the year when it is socially acceptable to say to your friends, "Let's go outside into the cold night and carol at the houses of strangers." All of this singing can take place only during the Advent season.

When we examine the events leading up to the birth of Christ, we see that indeed it was and is still a time of singing. St. Luke records four amazing and glorious songs surrounding the birth of God's Son.

The first song to consider is Zechariah's, which concerns the "amazing gift" of God to His people in the coming of His only Son, Jesus Christ. Luke records for us the surprising events of the announcement and birth of John the Baptist, our Lord's cousin and forerunner.

Zechariah and Elizabeth are considered too old to have children, yet God confounds the normal ways of humans and miraculously blesses Zechariah and Elizabeth with a boy. God silences Zechariah as a sign of His power until the day of circumcision, when the baby is to be named.

As soon as Zechariah acknowledges in faith and obedience to God that the child is to be named John, his tongue is freed and he praises God for all he is worth. He and Elizabeth marvel that they are blessed with a son who will prepare the way for the promised Messiah. The Holy Spirit fills Zechariah, and he breaks forth in jubilant song with words of praise and prophecy. This hymn of Zechariah is often called the "Benedictus," from the first words of the Latin translation of this Bible section: "Blessed be the Lord" (Lk 1:68).

The song of Zechariah may be called "Amazing Gift." In the words of this song, we see just how amazing the promised gift of God's Son becomes for us, His people.

THE AMAZING GIFT OF GOD COMES TO VISIT HIS PEOPLE

Zechariah begins his song with the words "Blessed be the Lord God of Israel, for He has visited and redeemed His people" (v. 68). We celebrate along with Zechariah the faithfulness of God. He did not forget His people! The Lord made a promise to send a Savior, and He fulfilled it. He established a covenant and maintained it. God swore an oath, and He kept it. God's salvation plan had been at work for thousands of years. All the way back at the time when Adam and Eve fell into sin, God could have wiped them off the face of the earth. Instead, God determined to send a Savior to bring humankind back into fellowship with Himself. The Savior would conquer Satan and give life back to God's people. In the coming of God's Son, Jesus Christ, we celebrate the fulfillment of God's promises. The apostle John reflects this same truth when he writes, "The Word became flesh and dwelt among us" (Jn 1:14). God made good on His word in coming to us!

It is said that Henry David Thoreau once spent an entire day in Walden Pond up to his neck in the water. His idea was to see and experience the world as a frog sees it. But Thoreau never became a frog! The miracle of incarnation is that God became a human being. He became one of us to redeem us, His people (v. 68). God visited us! If He had wanted to communicate to and save dogs, He would have become a dog. If He had wanted to save birds, He would have become a bird. The amazing thing about the gift of God that Zechariah sings is that God came for us—people like you and me. God laid aside His celestial robes to don the simple raiment of a man. Divinity clothed itself with dust. God visited us!

What will the One coming, the One who came, and the One who will come again do? The amazing song of Zechariah tells us that He will give us the strength of His salvation. V. 69 says, "[He] has raised up a horn of salvation for us." The horn is a symbol of victorious strength. The strong victory of God for His people would be won by the coming gift of God's Son, who would be born as a little baby in Bethlehem but who would also grow up to die on a cross and rise from the grave.

The strength of Christ's victory is real, and it is for us this Advent season. In the midst of the world's hopelessness and helplessness, Christ brings strength and salvation. God comes to visit us this Advent as we hear His Word and receive His Sacrament. Our faith in Christ is made firm! His strength becomes our strength! The amazing gift of God comes to visit us as God's people and to assure us of His salvation.

The Amazing Gift Comes
to Shine into Our Darkness

Have you noticed how dark it is these days? The Advent season of the Church Year is the darkest time of the year. The sun is low in the sky, the shadows are long, and the days are short. In fact, it is estimated that during the winter months up to half of the people in the northern hemisphere suffer from lack of light. The absence of light brings depression and despair. We need light!

Zechariah's amazing song reminds us that the gift of God comes to bring us what we need—light! In v. 78, God reminds us of His tender mercy, which is like the rising sun coming from heaven ("sunrise . . . from on high"). The gift of God will shine on those living in darkness and in the shadow of death (v. 79). John writes, "In Him was life, and the life was the light of men. The light shines in the darkness" (Jn 1:4–5).

We know about the darkness resulting from sin and its effect in our lives. This time of the year, perhaps more than at other times, our lives are filled with stress, worry, guilt, and fear. We try to please so many people and make up for things that we have done or failed to do in the past. We have this grand vision about what Christmas should be like, building false expectations about our holidays. Sure, we can try to cover ourselves by spending more than we should on that "perfect gift" for so-and-so. We can attempt to have perfect holiday parties and invite just the right people. We can cook all the right foods and plan to see all the right relatives. Yet, in the end, our lives can still be dark without the One who comes to fill us with the light and love of God.

Jesus Christ comes to dispel the darkness of sin and give us the light of His mercy. The amazing song of Zechariah reminds us of God's light in Christ, who shines into our dark places this Advent season. He exposes the darkness of our sinfulness and purifies us with His forgiveness. When light hits the darkness, the darkness is no more!

In the time leading up to Christmas we hear about letters to Santa. Once there was a little boy named Jimmy who wrote Santa just before Christmas: "Dear Santa, you didn't bring me anything good last year. And I don't remember anything good the year before either. This year will be your last chance. Signed, Jimmy."

The amazing gift of God sung about by Zechariah reminds us that God comes to bring us something wonderful. He comes to shine on our darkness and give us the light of His salvation. Jesus says, "I am the light of the world. Whoever follows Me will not walk in darkness, but will have the light of life" (Jn 8:12). Without Christ, we are living in the dark! With Him, we have the light of His life and forgiveness, which He won for us by His death and resurrection.

THE AMAZING GIFT COMES TO GUIDE OUR FEET

Since the coming gift of God in Jesus Christ is the light of the world, He also becomes a guide for us in our daily lives. Zechariah sings about how the One coming will "guide our feet into the way of peace" (v. 79).

The amazing thing about God becoming one of us in the person of His Son, Jesus Christ, is that He becomes our personal guide through life. As true man, Jesus experienced the same temptations and times of testing that we have in our lives. The big difference is that while we so often yield to Satan and his ways, Jesus stood firm. As the sinless Son of God, He walked a path of righteousness for us. By giving His life for us on the cross, He won for us redemption from sin, Satan, and death itself. He becomes the power source for our daily lives. Our Baptism into His name assures us that daily the old Adam is drowned so that the new man can come forth and live in God's renewed strength and power.

What would life be like without Christ as our guide? One time our family had the pleasure of touring Mammoth Cave National Park in Kentucky. While we had small flashlights on our helmets, after a while every part of the cave looked the same. At one point, the tour guide even had us turn off our lights. We would never have made it in the dark without that guide.

Sin blinds us to the path God would have us take. Yet Christ in His mercy lights a path for us! When we are discouraged or depressed, Christ fills us with His love. He helps us see a purpose to our lives as we live for Him who came for us and gave up His life as a ransom for us. God's grace keeps us from focusing on what we may get out of Christmas. Instead, the love of Christ moves us to find real joy and meaning in giving to others.

Zechariah's amazing song reminds us that the coming One brings a pathway of peace. Once again, this time of the year finds peace to be elusive in our world. Hot spots around the globe remain ready to become all-out war. Family members are at odds with one another. Our cities have been described as war zones themselves. Yet there is One who comes to bring true peace.

The peace Christ offers us is the result of what He, the Prince of Peace, came to do. By taking away our sins, He removed the wall of hostility between us and God. We have fellowship and harmony with Him because of what He has done for us. Our eternity is secure! Life makes sense because we know that God loves us and accepts the way that we are through the shed blood of His Son, Jesus Christ.

The slogan for a national bus line for many years has been "Leave the driving to us." Our Advent Lord and King, who guides us into His peace, invites us to trust Him for every aspect of our lives. What a comfort to know that we don't have to be our own driver. We can leave the driving and control of our lives in the hands of our Savior and guide. We trust Him for every aspect of life, knowing that He will give us all we need. As our Guide and Good Shepherd, He provides for us so that nothing or no one will ever be able to snatch us away from Him and His love.

During these weeks leading up to the celebration of Christ's birth, we will be hearing, humming, and singing familiar songs about the Savior who has come and is coming again. Wouldn't you agree that the amazing song of Zechariah concerning the gift of God in the coming of Christ is special and meaningful? May that song take root in our hearts this Advent as we praise God for His unspeakable gift: the gift who personally visits us as God's own people, the gift who shines into the darkness of our sins to bring the light and love of God, and the gift who guides us into the path of His perfect peace.

Advent 2

Mary's Song: Love

Luke 1:46–56

Some time ago, there was a news report about a young woman who had terrible indigestion and stomach pains. The pains worsened until finally she went to the doctor. There, in the doctor's office, she found out the reason for her pain. She gave birth to a healthy little girl. Can you imagine the surprise? We wonder how something like that could happen.

Certainly the month of December has facets of surprise built into it. The whole notion of giving and receiving gifts involves the element of surprise. About this time, parents are scrambling to find effective hiding places for gifts for those in the family who like to snoop! Children have attempted to get presents for each other and for their parents. Do you think they can keep the surprise?

During this Advent season we are watching the surprising, unfolding drama of the incarnation. As we are now in the second week of Advent, the time of Christ's birth is approaching. In this unfolding of the coming of Christ, we see many elements of surprise in God's undeserved and unexpected love.

One surprise was that Bethlehem was chosen as the place for Jesus to enter the world. There were bigger and grander towns, but God chose the humble little town of David's birth. Bethlehem was to be the town to experience the honor of God's grace and presence.

Then there was the surprise of Elizabeth's pregnancy at such an old age. Gabriel announced that Elizabeth would bear a son who would prepare the way for the ministry of the Messiah. When Elizabeth's husband, Zechariah, was informed, he doubted that God could really make this surprise happen. His doubts were literally silenced when God declared him mute until the baby was born!

Tonight we consider Mary's surprise—that God would choose a humble peasant teenager, who was unmarried, to give birth to the very Son of God.

The excitement and drama of Advent are great! The people God chose to play critical roles in fulfilling His promise were common people who were caught off guard by God's selection. We are told that Mary wondered and pondered and thought and prayed about this whole miracle of God's presence. She asks, "How will this be, since I am a virgin?" (Lk 1:34). Mary must have thought, "Are You really sure You want me? Lord, it seems too big, too grand, too important, too special for me to be chosen in Your amazing love and honored with Your presence!"

In the Gospel of Luke, we see how the amazing love of God left Mary both surprised and excited. God gave Mary a song about His surprising and amazing love. This song is often called the "Magnificat," from the first words of Mary in the Latin translation of this Bible portion. Mary begins her song with the words "My soul magnifies the Lord" (v. 46).

MARY MAGNIFIES GOD AND HIS LOVE

The amazing love of God was at work when the Lord chose Mary of all the women in the world to be the mother of His only Son. She didn't deserve to be chosen for this honor. She hadn't earned the right to bear the Christ Child. God chose her because of His mercy. Although Mary must have struggled with feelings of being unworthy, unprepared, and incapable, God's grace enabled her to accept His undeserving love. She faithfully comes to the point where she says, "Behold, I am the servant of the Lord; let it be to me according to Your word" (Lk 1:38). In response to God's amazing love, Mary breaks forth into her beautiful song of faith. She "magnifies" the Lord.

In our world today, the microchip is almost taken for granted. When it is magnified, though, we see hundreds and thousands of little lines, circuits, and patterns inscribed on its surface. These carry thousands of bits of information, bringing about technological miracles. When magnified, the microchip becomes highly significant.

Mary sings, "My soul magnifies the Lord." In response to God's amazing love, Mary "makes large" (magnifies) God's power and presence in choosing her to be part of His plan of salvation. Even though God's salvation plan had been at work for perhaps four thousand years, people had forgotten. They were not magnifying the Lord but instead were exalting themselves and their own ways. The angel Gabriel comes to Mary and says, "Greetings, O favored one, the Lord is with you!

. . . You will conceive in your womb and bear a son, and you shall call His name Jesus [Savior]. . . . He will reign over the house of Jacob forever, and of His kingdom there will be no end" (Lk 1:28, 31–33).

The example of Mary causes us to ask ourselves, "Who or what am I magnifying as I prepare for Christ to come?" Mary sings, "He who is mighty has done great things for me, and holy is His name" (v. 49). Likewise, we can declare the same truth for ourselves. God has done great things for us in choosing us to be His own. He made us and then remade us through our Savior, Jesus Christ. Life and salvation are ours through God's amazing love given to us in the person of His Son to redeem us from our sins and assure us of eternal life.

Mary magnifies the Lord and His amazing love. To magnify the Lord means getting ourselves out of the way. It means focusing our faith and confidence on Christ, not on what we have done or can do. Yet the truth of the matter is that often we are in the business of magnifying ourselves. Look specifically at Mary's words in v. 51. "He has shown strength with His arm; He has scattered the proud in the thoughts of their hearts."

God opposes us when you and I elevate ourselves above Him and His grace. We want to take credit for our lives and how we have arrived. But we only fool ourselves! We fail to give credit to the Lord for what He has done in our lives. And God warns us that He opposes this kind of sinful pride.

A story is told about a man who went with his wife to an arcade. He saw one of those scales where you place a quarter into a slot and you receive your weight along with a little message on a card. He put his quarter in and weighed himself, and out popped the card. The card read: "You are handsome and gregarious, and people think much of you. You will be a very great success." With smugness and pride, he handed the card to his wife and said, "See, look at what this says about me." His wife took the card and read it. She looked at him and then at the scale and then back at him. With bland candor she retorted, "Yep, it even got your weight wrong."

Tonight, as we look at the message of Mary's song of amazing love, we need to recognize ourselves for who we are. We are sinful human beings who apart from the grace of God deserve only death. God is holy, and we are not! Mary truly recognized this. She admitted that she was a humble servant. She declared that she was unworthy of all the honor that God had bestowed on her. She understood that the God of grace would be sending her what she also needed—a Savior.

A profound truth came across my desk the other day when I read these words: "Do you realize that only the small birds sing?" It is not the proud and mighty eagles that sing. You may hear them screech, but you have never heard them utter a note in song. Yet you have heard the little sparrows, the clearly marked robins, and the bright cardinals sing melodious tunes. The tiny birds are the ones with songs rather than the mighty and majestic. It is when you and I are small and humble before God, like Mary, that He gives us a song of His amazing love. We understand that we are chosen and redeemed solely by His grace and not by anything we do.

GOD MAGNIFIES US IN HIS LOVE

We know that the baby given to Mary, whom she praises in her song of amazing love, is our Savior as well. Like Mary, we can be surprised at the honor of God's amazing love. You and I have been chosen to have the honor of Christ's very presence this Christmas. Despite our pride and sins of self-sufficiency, God still loves us. Indeed, He magnifies each of us with His undeserved love. Truly, "He who is mighty has done great things for me" (v. 49). Isn't it amazing that even though God knows us perfectly and sees all our sins, He still cares?

We need to hear this good news once again this Advent and Christmas. All around us, we are beaten down by the gloom and doom of the world. We are well aware of economic threats to ourselves and our families. We know about crime statistics and layoffs and restructuring and cutbacks. We know all about sickness and cancer and heart attacks. We experience the depression of letdowns and broken human relationships. In fact, it is difficult for some people to see anything good about God's amazing love at Christmas. One person asked me, "Aren't you happy that Christmas comes only once a year?" Walking behind a woman at a mall, I overheard her say, "I wish we could just do away with Christmas!" Many people are tired and worn-out and just plain bored with the whole Christmas scene.

Not only are people bored with Christmas, but there are many who are tired of God. Their faith is routine and lacks excitement. Worship is seen as dull and boring. They only come out of obligation at certain times of the year, like at Christmas and Easter. Many people find their walk with God to be boring. They do not understand God's amazing love in His Son, Jesus Christ. God's powerful Word has been rejected in their heart so that God's amazing love has not been magnified.

In v. 50, Mary declares that God is not only holy but also merciful. "His mercy is for those who fear Him from generation to generation." The Lord tonight extends His mercy to us. He came to us in the person of His Son to be born, to die on a cross, to rise again from the grave, and to give us victory over Satan, sin, and death. The gift of God's Son adds meaning and vitality to life because we know that we are forgiven. His amazing love gives us a purpose—to live not just for ourselves but for Him who loved us and purchased us with His shed blood. Truly, God magnifies us with His undeserved and amazing love!

We Magnify God's Amazing Love

In response to God's love, we, like Mary, magnify Him. We make Him large in our hearts and our lives. We give Him praise and glory in acknowledging Him as the one who came as our Savior, who comes to us every day as our merciful Lord, and who promises to come again at the end of time to take us to be with Him. But how do we magnify Him during this Advent season?

In Mary's song of God's amazing love, she faithfully praises God for His care and compassion. She sings, "He has shown strength with His arm" (v. 51); "He has filled the hungry with good things" (v. 53); "He has helped His servant Israel, in remembrance of His mercy" (v. 54). Like Mary, we praise and thank God in faith for providing for all our needs. As we look back on this past year, each of us can point to mighty deeds that God has performed in our lives. The simple things we take for granted; the everyday blessings like food, shelter, and clothing; the daily care and preservation he provides—for all this and more, we magnify God's amazing love.

There is a story of a single mother and her young son during the Great Depression. It was especially difficult for them to make ends meet during the winter months. Specifically, they did not have enough money to pay for both food to eat and coal to heat their house. Difficult decisions had to be made. In order to stay warm at night, the two of them slept in the same bed. They kept warm as the mother heated boards in the oven and then wrapped them with newspapers found on the street. The warm boards wrapped in paper made the cold nights bearable. One night as they were getting ready for bed, the little boy looked at his mother and said, "Mom, I feel so sorry for kids who don't have warm boards and paper." A story like this makes us appreciate what we have.

A song like Mary's points us to God's goodness and love so that we are moved to thanksgiving. God certainly provides for us. And so we trust Him and thank Him. Even if we can point to nothing specific for which to be thankful (I would find this hard to believe), we still magnify the Lord because He has forgiven our sins and rescued us from the pit of hell for the glory of heaven. Like Mary, we have a song to sing! God has considered our lives. He has addressed our problems. He has redeemed us from our sins.

How do we magnify God's amazing love? Like Mary, we have a song of witness to share with the world. And we sing it aloud! Magnifying the Lord means telling others about Him. When people are truly thankful and proud of something that has happened in their lives, they usually want to talk about it. Have you ever listened to yourself when you are excited about something? You want to make sure people hear about it. Why don't we do the same with God? Why don't we say, "World, listen up! Listen to what my God did!" But this is exactly what Mary did.

She magnified the Lord because He had done great things in her life. She spoke out! She let people know!

This is what Christmas is all about. It is about telling people of God's amazing love—busting our buttons over God and His goodness. After all, when is a more receptive time for people of the world to hear the message of Christ Jesus? People are talking about Christmas and God's Son. They are open to Him and His love. Everywhere you go, people are tuned in. Why not talk about the God who gives us a reason to sing songs, to give gifts, and to put up lights on the most precarious places of our homes? We magnify the Lord along with Mary and innumerable other witnesses throughout the centuries, testifying to the amazing love of God in Christ Jesus.

Mary was certainly surprised when God chose her to be the mother of His Son, our Savior. God's undeserved amazing love is often unexpected and surprising. Yet this Advent and Christmas we magnify God along with Mary for the great things He has done for us. Most of all, we praise Him for the life and salvation He gives to us through His Son, who comes to us again this year. Together, we respond in thankful praise for all He has done for us. We trust Him to continue to bless us and give us what we truly need. And we magnify the Lord, speaking a witness to all who will listen, telling them about God's amazing love.

Advent 3

Simeon's Song: Amazing Peace

Luke 2:25–35

Years ago, a man was soliciting door-to-door for a Christian orphanage. The solicitor approached one exasperated homemaker and asked, "Would you like to give a donation to the Lutheran Children's Orphanage?" The man was surprised when the woman said, "Yes, wait a minute, and I'll get them—they are ages 2 and 4!"

Parents of young children may have moments of exasperation, yet we understand that our children are indeed gifts from God. During this final week before the celebration of our Lord's birth, we take time out from our busy schedules to recognize the greatest gift of God—the gift of His Son, Jesus Christ, who came as our Savior at Bethlehem, who comes to us this very evening to give us His peace and presence, and who promises to come again as our triumphant Lord and King.

One of the gifts God brings to us this Advent is the gift of peace. During the Christmas season, many people talk about peace. We sing, "Peace on earth and mercy mild, God and sinners reconciled!" (*LSB* 380:1). But how many people really have true peace? How many times have you wished for peace of mind? And have we not all desired peace in our souls—that is, peace with God? It is a shame that we often reserve the phrase "peace with God" as something that only happens to people on their deathbeds.

This evening we examine the song of Simeon, an aged man in the temple. His song might be titled "Amazing Peace." The song of Simeon reminds us that we don't "make peace." God did and still does! How does the Lord give us His peace?

True Peace Comes as a Result of Knowing and Trusting in God's Salvation through Christ

In our Scripture lesson, we read that Simeon was a righteous and devout man (Lk 2:25). He trusted in God and His promise to send a Savior. In the temple, Simeon had been waiting and waiting for God to make good on His promise. He had been waiting for God to deliver the Prince of Peace.

We are told by our text that Simeon had to wait no longer. Jesus had been brought by Mary and Joseph, after the time of her purification, to be consecrated to the Lord according to the Law of the Lord. While they were there, the Holy Spirit led Simeon to Jesus and His parents. Simeon took little Jesus in his arms and broke into a song of praise to God.

God led Simeon to understand that the little baby he was holding was the Prince of Peace, the one chosen by God to save the world. He sings, "Lord, now You are letting Your servant depart in peace, according to Your word; for my eyes have seen Your salvation" (vv. 29–30). Simeon was led by God to know and trust that in Christ, God was making peace with humankind. Through this child that Simeon held up, God would give to His people a peace of heart, mind, and soul that could be found nowhere else. Most of all, the peace of God was now Simeon's. He had seen with his own eyes the promised salvation of God. We can only imagine the joy and peace that Simeon experienced as a result of God's making good on His promise to send the Savior.

Make no mistake, the peace that Simeon found in the Christ Child would not come easy. As Simeon hands the child back to Mary and Joseph, he tells them from God that while many will be raised up as they trust in Him for life and peace, there would also be suffering. "A sword will pierce through your own soul also" (v. 35), Simeon spoke. This is the first reference in the Gospel of Luke that the salvation and peace Jesus came to bring would come only through a cross. Mary and Jesus would suffer great anguish as Christ would suffer and die for the sins of the world.

During this week before Christmas, it is hard to find people who are at peace with themselves, God, or other people. Even though we replay the Christmas message each year and talk about "peace on earth, goodwill toward men," we just don't see much of it in living color. The peace that Christ brings not only seems to pass people's understanding—it passes many people by completely. We've become so busy that the pace of life overshadows the purpose of life, so that there is no peace in our own lives.

We know that Christmas is a difficult time for many. Suicides are up and many people are down. They come up empty in their search for real and lasting peace and joy. In a few days, the presents will all be unwrapped, but the happiness will be worn off. All that remains is a pile of bills. In this next week, the Christmas frenzy will build to a crescendo, but it will soon all be over. Still there is no peace.

In the temple with Simeon, there were, no doubt, many busy people hustling and bustling around. They missed out on the peace that Simeon found! Are we so busy with the externals of Christmas that we miss the gift of peace? Are we trying to find peace in the perfect gifts, the right company, financial security?

One time I attended an exciting football game. As the most crucial play of the game was about to occur, my wife asked me a question about something here at church. I turned my head to answer her and missed what turned out to be the turning point of the game. If we miss the peace of Jesus Christ this Christmas, we miss much more than an important football play. If we let Christmas slip by without knowing and trusting (like Simeon) in the peace of Christ, which He won for us on the cross of Calvary, we miss out completely on the peace of heart, mind, and soul that Jesus Christ came to bring.

God's Peace Brings His Presence for All of Life

It is rather amazing that even though Simeon had been waiting for years for God to make good on His promise to send a Savior, he didn't give up. He still had confidence that God would make good on His word. V. 25 tells us that Simeon was "waiting for the consolation of Israel, and the Holy Spirit was upon him." We can only imagine that he had a twinkle in his eye as he expected God's abundant blessing through the coming of the Christ Child.

In faith, do we expect the blessing of God's presence and peace for our lives? The color blue reminds us of the Advent hope that we have in Christ. Our hope in Christ and the peace He comes to bring is more than just wishful thinking. Our hope is based on the sure promises of God! Along with Simeon, since we have seen by faith the salvation of the Lord in Christ Jesus, we can be dismissed to go out into the world in peace.

Even though Simeon at this point in his life may have had dimmed vision and difficulty in hearing, God opened his eyes and ears to the fulfillment of His promises in Christ. This evening as we hear God's Word of promise, He opens our eyes, our ears, and our hearts so that we can confidently know and expect God's blessings. Christ's coming assures us that our sins are forgiven. The abundant life Christ brings is ours, so that in Him we have no need for anxious worry. Paul writes in Phil 4:6–7: "Do not be anxious about anything, but in everything by prayer and supplication with thanksgiving let your requests be made known to God. And the peace of God, which surpasses all understanding, will guard your hearts and your minds in Christ Jesus."

A man and his grandson were walking on the beach one day when they met an old man. They stopped and talked to him. As they talked, it seemed that nothing in his life was any good to this man. His grandchildren ignored him. He hadn't had a very good lunch. The fish weren't biting. And to top it all off, he said he was suffering from sunstroke. The little boy listened to the conversation, and as they continued their walk, he said, "Granddad, I hope you never suffer from a sunset."

Simeon certainly had not suffered from a sunset as he waited on God to make good on His promises. He knew that he could trust God to come through. Our faith is firmed up during the Advent season as we are assured of the presence and peace of God to sustain us in all of life. We never suffer from a "Son-set." For the One who came still comes to us every day. He gives a vitality and meaning to our life. His grace is sufficient for all of our needs. The peace of His presence enables us to live each day to the fullest, to His glory.

GOD'S PEACE IN CHRIST BECOMES A WITNESS TO THE WORLD

As Simeon holds the Christ Child and praises God in his amazing song of peace, he declares that this gift of God's peace will be "a light for revelation to the Gentiles" (v. 32). God reminds us in this song of Simeon that the peace of God in Jesus Christ is not just for a certain group of people. The mercy of God in Christ is for everyone! Forgiveness of sins, life, and salvation are offered to all through the person and work of Jesus Christ.

The Advent and Christmas season is a special time of the year for us Christians. It is one of the few times during the year that the world gives us the license to carry our message of peace and hope to our families, our communities, and the world. By the songs we sing, the decorations we put up, the words we speak, and the actions we display, we witness to the world concerning the love and peace of our Savior and King.

This year we completed our nativity scene here at church. It has been interesting to hear the comments of people in the neighborhood. One woman said, "Every time I go by your church, I am reminded of the real meaning of Christmas." Watching out my office window, I've seen people with children get out of their cars, walk up to the manger, and closely examine the figures. To some this is such a little thing, yet by God's grace our nativity scene becomes a witness to our community.

In our conversations with our relatives, neighbors, and friends, we let them know the real reason for this season of peace. "What will you be doing for Christmas?" is a question you will be asked at the office or by your neighbors. What will you say? Will you reply that you and your family will be worshiping the God who came to be our Savior? Will you share how important it is that you and your family are focused on Jesus Christ as the one who came, who lived and died and rose, and who promises to come again?

When the famous Christian missionary William Carey was home on furlough, he was given a standing ovation after speaking at a banquet. The program leader went on to the next speaker, but before that speaker could begin his address, Carey leaped to the center of the stage and cried, "Aren't you going to do anything about it?"

The peace of Christ Jesus doesn't simply come to us. It also goes through us! In response to the life-giving eternal peace we have in our hearts and lives, we become witnesses like Simeon. Simeon declared the light of God's peace in Christ to all in the temple who would listen. God's peace and presence in us moves us to become witnesses this Advent and Christmas season in our words and actions.

Above the door to our sanctuary is a sign that reads: "Enter to Worship, Exit to Witness." Simeon came to the temple that day long ago to worship the God who had promised to send a Savior who would give him perfect peace. He left the temple that same day having held the Promised One of God, the Messiah, the Lord Jesus Christ. In true faith, this Advent and Christmas, we behold Christ once again as the Savior who gives us life and salvation. We worship the God who keeps His promises! But we cannot leave as we came.

This Advent and Christmas, we will hear a lot about peace. While the world sings about peace and talks about peace, we know and trust in the peace that God came to bring us in the person of His Son, Jesus Christ. Like Simeon, may the peace of Christ fill your heart and mind. May His peace bring you the assurance and comfort of His forever presence. And may His peace move you to become a powerful witness for Him.

Christmas Eve

The Angels' Song: Amazing Glory

Luke 2:8–15

Tonight the world pauses to celebrate! Yes, and everything you were supposed to get done has been accomplished. The gifts have all been wrapped (and many unwrapped). The company has arrived. The kids are home from college. The stores are closed. That special Christmas Eve meal has been prepared and eaten. And now we can sit back and pause to reflect on the real reason for our celebration. The angel of the Lord announces to us along with the shepherds, "Fear not, for behold, I bring you good news of a great joy that will be for all the people. For unto you is born this day in the city of David a Savior, who is Christ the Lord" (Lk 2:10–11).

This year in our Advent preparations we have been looking at the various songs leading up to and including the birth of our Savior. Tonight our Christmas songs come to a crescendo. Luke tells us that as the shepherds heard about the birth of the Savior in Bethlehem, the Savior wrapped in cloths and lying in a manger, there was suddenly a great company of heavenly host praising God and singing, "Glory to God in the highest, and on earth peace among those with whom He is pleased!" (v. 14).

It was a common practice that when a baby boy was born in those days, local musicians would congregate at the child's house to greet him with simple music. Jesus was born in a stable in a town unfamiliar to his parents and their friends. Yet how amazing that the minstrels of heaven took the place of the minstrels of earth as the angels sang a song of glory at the birth of Christ. What a scene that must have been! All heaven broke forth in glorifying and praising God.

We have titled the song of the angels "Amazing Glory." The foremost of God's invisible creation, the angels, were so excited about the new relationship of God with His people that they praised God with everything they had. They glorified God!

To give God glory is to honor Him. To give Him glory is to hold Him in the highest possible esteem. To ascribe glory to God is to acknowledge that the Lord is supreme—above all. He is the powerful Creator and ruler of the universe, who was determined in the gracious act of sending His one and only Son to rescue humankind from its sins. The loving act of sending His only Son to become a man in order to bring us back to God describes the awesome glory and honor due His name tonight.

As we celebrate the true meaning of Christmas, we also glorify God as the angels did. We praise Him this evening along with the multitude of the heavenly host. Why do we give glory to God?

GOD'S GLORY REFLECTS GOD'S GRACE

There was a European monarch who worried other officials by disappearing and walking incognito among his people. When he was asked not to do so for security's sake, he answered, "I cannot rule my people unless I know how they live." The grace of God is shown clearly by God's becoming one of us. In the coming of Jesus Christ we have a God who knows the life we live because He, too, lived it. He is Immanuel—God with us! He came to become one of us.

We did not deserve this grace. On the contrary, the God who created us has the right to expect us to live according to His glory. Yet we know the reality of our situation. Rom 3:23 reminds us that we all have "fall[en] short of the glory of God." In our thoughts, words, and actions, we do not live up to what our Maker has a right to expect of us. The Bible calls this "sin." We miss the mark of God's glory! The cold and darkness at this time of the year remind us of the bleak situation of our hearts and lives by nature. Yet the amazing glory of God is centered tonight on His grace—His undeserved love for us.

Perhaps you've heard the story about the man stopping on his way home from work at the supermarket to do a little shopping. All he needs is a loaf of bread and a gallon of milk. He is standing in the checkout line. Behind him is a woman with a cart full of groceries and two small kids tugging at her leg. At the man's turn at the register, the clerk invites him to pull the winning number out of a fishbowl. "If you pull out the winning number, then all your groceries are free," the clerk explains.

The bowl is so full that the chances are slim, but the fellow tries anyway. Wouldn't you know it? He gets the winning ticket! What a surprise! Then he looks at his cart with only a loaf of bread and some milk. What a waste! But this fellow is quick. He turns to the woman behind him—the one with the mountain of groceries—and says, "Well, what do you know, honey? We won! We don't have to pay a penny." She looks at him, and he winks. She steps up beside him, puts her arm around him, and smiles.

We, too, have been graced with a surprise. Like the woman, we have been given a gift. The good news of the great joy of God's grace is that "unto [us] is born this day in the city of David a Savior, who is Christ the Lord." The gift of God's grace is not for us at the checkout stand, but at the judgment seat of God.

We sing along with the angels, "Glory to God in the highest!" He loves us tonight with an everlasting grace. Despite our sins, He comes to us to be born in us as our Savior. He grew up to die on a cross in our place. He rose from the grave after three days to win the victory over Satan and sin and even death. God made good on His plan to save us and to give us all that we need in this life and for eternity. Indeed, glory to God!

God's Glory Brings Peace

As we look at the angels' song, we see that they sang, "Glory to God in the highest, and on earth peace among those with whom He is pleased" (v. 14).

When people are asked what they would like for Christmas, so many desire peace. We want to have peace in our families, peace in our world, peace in our nation, and peace in our own hearts. Many people say they especially enjoy Christmas Eve worship. By now so many of the cultural and social events of Christmas are over. Parents, grandparents, and finally all of us can sit back and breathe a sigh of relief, knowing that everything that was supposed to be done has been done. We can finally sit back and focus on the gift of gifts, God's Son, come to be our Savior. As the angels promised in their song of amazing glory, the One born for us this evening comes to bring peace. God's grace and glory bring us His peace.

The oldest member of Carmel Lutheran Church is 99 years old, soon to be 100. She is in a retirement home. She can't hear very well. Her eyes can't see the fine print anymore. Yet God has enabled her still to be sharp in her mind. She has outlived all of her friends and most of her family. She still has one daughter living. I asked her recently how she would be spending Christmas. She says that this year, like her years stretching into the last century, she will sit down and read the Christmas Gospel from Luke 2. She will read about how God made good on His promise to send a Savior. She will remember how this little baby grew up to die on a cross for her and to rise again to take away her sins. God's grace will enable her by faith to receive the peace of the Lord Jesus Christ into her heart and life once again.

She told me that this simple time with God is what really "makes" her Christmas and brings her peace. What is it that will "make" your Christmas this year and truly give you God's peace? If the Lord wills, you also may gaze backward to earlier years in your life. What really matters to you won't be the condition of your house and whether or not you vacuumed up the Christmas tree needles one last time. It will not matter what gifts you gave or received. You probably won't remember the food you ate. What will matter is the eternal peace that you have graciously been given by God through His Son, Jesus Christ.

God offers to us tonight, through His Word and Sacrament, the peace to know that our sins are completely forgiven. We have the peace of our Savior to know that even if everything went wrong in a worldly way this Christmas, God still cares for us and has a good plan for our lives. We have the peace of Christ to experience and to let overflow in our relationships with others. His glory and grace give us the peace to reach out in love to others as God loves us. And finally, we have the peace of God in Christ to know that one day, when our life on this earth ends, we, too, shall join "with angels and archangels and with all the company of heaven [as] we laud and magnify [His] glorious name" (*LSB Altar Book*, p. 264). We praise God for His glorious peace!

GOD'S GLORY IS RECOGNIZED BY TRUE FAITH

God's presence and peace are offered to us again this Christmas. Unfortunately, the attitude of so many today reflects the feelings of the common folk of Bethlehem. There is just no time, no room for Jesus to be born for them. Satan and sin continually want to shut Jesus out! We are tempted to think that we can handle life all by ourselves without God's glorious presence.

The Word of the Lord came to the shepherds, announcing the "good news of a great joy" (v. 10). The multitude of heavenly host sang their glorious song. And we are told that the shepherds listened. God gave the lowly shepherds the grace to follow His instructions. We are told that they went with haste and found Mary and Joseph and the baby Jesus, just as God had told them through the angel. They worshiped Him and acknowledged Him as the promised Savior of the world. Even though the world despised them as unclean and unworthy of God's love and favor, those shepherds trusted in God's Son as the one who would love them just as they were. God gave them the faith to accept His peace and hope. They were able to glorify God along with the angels for the peace that God's Promised One had come to bring as He would take their sins upon a cross and die and rise for them to give them eternal life.

We celebrate with the angels and the shepherds this evening as by grace we receive Jesus Christ by faith. Along with the shepherds and all others who have gone before us in true faith, we make room for the Lord Jesus Christ in our hearts and lives. Christmas must be more than sentimentality, more than getting together by a fireplace and sitting around a beautifully decorated tree. Our response to God's grace and glory must be more than exchanging gifts. Ultimately, Christmas is about receiving the One who came as a baby, who then went to a cross to die for our sins, who rose again from the grave. Ultimately, the Christmas glory we celebrate directs our hearts and minds to the One who promises and bestows eternal salvation to all who place their trust in Him.

In faith we listen again this year to the good news of great joy. In true faith we respond like the shepherds to behold Christ as our personal Savior from sin and death. In faith we will come to the altar in a few minutes to receive the very body and blood of Christ our Lord, under and with the bread and wine, for the forgiveness of our sins and strengthening of our faith.

We thank God for all of you here this evening. Along with the angels, we sing songs of glory to Christ, our newborn King. We also pray that this Christ is someone with whom you can have a personal relationship of faith all year long. Christ Jesus is the one we glorify and worship for more than just one night a year. Our Savior is someone we trust in for more than a day or season. He is our glorious Lord for eternity. In response for what He has done for us, we want to make room for Him by faith in our hearts and lives all year long!

What does it mean to recognize the glory of God in Jesus Christ this Christmas? Let me summarize the true story about a fatherless family at Christmastime told in the book *Christmas in My Heart* by Dr. Joe L. Wheeler. The family had been well off until the husband left a note to say good-bye—leaving a wife, three small girls, and an empty bank account. The mother, named Mary, had tried to start a new life by cleaning houses. It kept the family off of welfare, and the girls were fed. They all wore clothes handed down from Mary's employers' children. They did not have a car, so they had to walk everywhere.

Mary walked the two oldest girls to school every day and then headed to the house she was to clean. She took with her the youngest, named Becky. Becky found happiness in her doll, which she named Charlie. That doll was her whole world. She dressed Charlie for the weather and then wrapped him in his precious blanket. It was just an old scrap of a blanket that somebody had dropped in a parking lot; Becky found it there, Mary washed it, and now it was Charlie's.

As Christmas approached, the large homes Mary cleaned were ready for the season. The two older girls knew there would be no Christmas tree for them—just like last year. Money was not to be spent on anything they could do without. And it hurt!

Little Becky oohed and aahed over all the fancy Christmas decorations. After spending a week at the various houses decked out in glorious fashion, Becky suddenly realized that she was missing out on something. "Why does everyone have a tree in the house, Mama? Why are there so many presents? Is it somebody's birthday? Why don't we have a tree?"

Mary pulled Becky onto her lap. "You're a very smart girl," she said. "It is somebody's birthday, and I'll tell you about Him. His name is Jesus, and He was born Christmas Day." Mary told all three girls how it came to happen and why there is a Christmas. Becky hugged her doll, Charlie, close. "Ooh, the poor baby. Was it very cold in the stable? I wouldn't want to sleep in a stable, would you? I wish I could go and see it, though." Mary immediately took the girls for a walk down the street to a church where a large crèche was set up. The girls were awed by the simple but beautiful scene. It was just like their mom had said.

The week before Christmas was difficult. While parents loaded up with the latest computer games and toys, Mary picked out economy packs of socks and underwear for the girls' gifts. At the grocery store, she whipped through the express lane with one lone box of spaghetti for their Christmas dinner as she glimpsed at the long lines of people with their carts full of turkeys and fixings. Mary tried not to notice, but she hurt inside as families strapped the perfect trees to the roofs of their cars. Bitterness grew inside Mary's heart when the two older girls came home from school telling about how they avoided all the other kids who made fun of them at recess.

Every carol and decoration and Christmas card made her hate the season more. Only little Becky was immune. She rocked Charlie in her arms and told him again and again about baby Jesus, who was born in a stable. She begged her mom to take her by the church so she could see the baby again.

Christmas morning came, and the two older girls came into their mother's bedroom. "I'm afraid there aren't a lot of gifts for you girls, but go and wake up Becky and you can open what there is." Too soon, they were back. "Where is Becky, Mama? We can't find her!" Frantically, they looked all around the house, and also at the neighbors' houses. Then Mary noticed Charlie. Charlie was never out of Becky's sight. And where was Charlie's blanket? Suddenly she knew!

Down the street Mary ran, until she could see the church. As she neared the church, tears of relief ran down her face as she caught a glimpse of her daughter. The star from the crèche was shining down on the manger, where Becky had climbed in and was busily covering the baby Jesus with the ratty scrap of her blanket.

Mary could hear Becky talking. "You must be cold," Becky said to the figure of baby Jesus in the manger. "This is Charlie's blanket, but we will give it to you." About then, Becky saw her mother. "I was afraid He might have thought we forgot about Him on His birthday."

Mary plucked Becky out of the straw and held her tight, the tears now raining unchecked. "I did forget, honey. . . . Dear Lord, I'm sorry I forgot." Then she tenderly carried her daughter home, filled at last with Christmas joy.

This night, we can't forget! God comes to us! Immanuel—truly God is with us! And along with the angels and the shepherds, and all the faithful believers of the past, we praise God for the glory of His grace, which comes to us so clearly tonight. We once again joyfully receive His peace, which He won for us by His coming, His death on the cross, and His resurrection. And tonight we make room in our hearts and lives for our Lord and Savior, Jesus Christ, on this, His birthday.

Mary

Rev. Arthur A. Just Jr.

Advent 1

Mary's Catechesis— The Annunciation

Luke 1:26–38

One of the surprises for many of us as we read the first chapter of Luke's Gospel is the prominent place of Mary in the story of Jesus' birth. Mary appears as an Old Testament saint who receives good news from an angel. A Jewish audience of Luke's Gospel would be struck how Jewish this Gospel appears as the narrative unfolds. Luke begins by introducing us to two aged Old Testament saints, Zechariah and Elizabeth. The miraculous circumstances of John's birth resemble the miraculous birth of Isaac to two aged saints, Abraham and Sarah, and the birth of Samuel to Elkanah and Hannah. And what could be more Jewish than the liturgical rhythm of the temple with its sacrificial offerings?

An angel greets this insignificant virgin from Nazareth, who scholars estimate could have been no more than 15 years old! In the announcement from the angel Gabriel, Mary learns what God is doing to redeem our lost and fallen race. This is Mary's catechesis, that is, where the Lord speaks to her through the angel about the miraculous child she will conceive in her womb by the Holy Spirit, and where she echoes back in humble, trusting faith, "Let it be to me according to Your word" (v. 38).

THE SETTING FOR HER CATECHESIS

The evangelist Luke sets the scene by introducing the circumstances of this miraculous event. The angel Gabriel appears to Mary, a virgin betrothed to Joseph of the house of David, in Nazareth of Galilee, during the sixth month of Elizabeth's pregnancy. Very little is said about Mary herself except her relationship to Joseph. Her insignificance and her humble circumstances are arresting. The only significant piece of information is her status as "virgin," which is repeated twice to emphasize this state.

The action of the angel's announcement to Mary is also very simple. Gabriel comes to Mary to tell her that she will soon carry within her body the Lord Himself. Mary is deeply troubled by the word and greeting of Gabriel. But the angel alleviates her fear by stating that Mary's condition comes from God because she has found favor with Him. And the miraculous birth is announced!

THE CONTENT OF CATECHESIS IS ABOUT JESUS CHRIST

The greeting of the angel to Mary is simply "The Lord is with you" (v. 28). The Lord is with Mary in two senses. He will come upon her and overshadow her, and the Lord will be in her womb. With this conception begins the new era of salvation. Luke contrasts this to Zechariah and Elizabeth, whose son, John the Baptist, is born according to the old era with its laws and regulations. The new era of salvation will now come through the womb of Mary, and this will only happen through the gracious action of God upon Mary, who finds favor with God because God chooses to bestow His favor on her.

Is this not the same with us as we are incorporated into the Kingdom by the pure grace of God? As Eve contained in her womb all humanity that was doomed to sin, now Mary contains in her womb a new humanity that is promised grace because of her Son, Jesus Christ. Thus the angel says, "Rejoice," for Israel is now reborn through Mary's womb. The Lord is with Mary—He is with His Church—He is with you and me!

Mary is instructed by the angel concerning the child whom she will conceive and bear. This is her catechesis! Titles for this child abound: He is called Jesus, Son of the Most High, King, and Son of God. For the audience of Luke's Gospel, there should be no doubt at this point who is the subject of this Gospel. Although Luke does not give us the meaning of the name "Jesus" (1:31), Matthew does: "He will save His people from their sins" (Mt 1:21). The Old Testament equivalent is Joshua, i.e., deliverer, savior. It sums up both the person and work of the Messiah. John the Baptist will be "great before the Lord" (Lk 1:15), but Jesus is great, the Son of the Most High (1:32).

The annunciation of the angel Gabriel to Mary is a day to be marked, for on this day the Kingdom comes, because Jesus is a continuation of the Davidic line. All the promises of God in the Old Testament are now coming to fulfillment in Christ, and specifically the promise of an everlasting kingdom to the house of David: "The Lord God will give to Him the throne of His father David, and He will reign over the house of Jacob forever, and of His kingdom there will be no end" (1:32–33). The royal line of the kingdom of Judah, prophesied by Jacob (Genesis 49), merges with the royal line of David (2 Sam 7:16): "And your house and your kingdom shall be made sure forever before Me. Your throne shall be established forever." Jesus is now a king who will reign over the house of David, because the messianic and kingly succession now continues in Jesus.

MARY AS THE FIRST CATECHUMEN

The climax of the angel's words is the announcement that the Virgin will conceive a child by the power of the Holy Spirit. Mary asks the angel, "How will this be, since I am a virgin?" (1:34). The angel responds, "The Holy Spirit will come upon you, and the power of the Most High will overshadow you" (v. 35). This is the same Spirit who hovered over the waters and brought forth creation (Gen 1:2), who hung over Israel as the presence of God in the pillar of cloud (the *shekinah*) during the exodus (Exodus 13, 14, 33), who covered the ark of the covenant (Exodus 40) and Mount Sinai (Exodus 19). This same Spirit descended on Jesus at His Baptism (Luke 3), hid Him in the cloud at His transfiguration (Luke 9), and clothed His disciples with power from on high (Lk 24:49). As the Holy Spirit comes upon Mary and overshadows her, she conceives Jesus as holy, the Son of God.

Luther always maintained that the conception of Jesus came through the power of God's word in Mary's ear. She heard the word from the angel and conceived the child. Mary is truly the first catechumen, since catechumens were called "hearers of the Word." This child conceived in Mary by the power of the Holy Spirit is the incarnate God, greater than Isaac or Samuel, greater than His cousin John. "Holy" and "Son of God" are the final titles given to Jesus (v. 35). At Jesus' Baptism and again at His transfiguration, the Father confirms that Jesus is "My beloved Son" (Lk 3:22), telling us what we already know from Jesus' conception.

The Nicene Creed captures all the teaching of the incarnation in a single phrase: Jesus "was incarnate by the Holy Spirit of the virgin Mary and was made man." As "Son of God" and "holy," Jesus is set apart by God to cleanse Israel—and all of us—from our sins and to inherit for us the Kingdom promised by the Father.

The coming of the Holy Spirit upon Mary reminds us of the descent of the Spirit on Jesus at His Baptism and the gift of the Holy Spirit we received at our Baptism. When the power of the Most High overshadows her, God becomes incarnate—becomes flesh—as part of her flesh, reminding us of the reception of the body and blood of Christ into the believer's body in the Lord's Supper. This is our first glimpse of the pattern of incorporation into the Church that Luke traces throughout Luke and Acts and in the early Christian communities: catechesis, Baptism, and the Lord's Supper. Mary prefigures all this as she receives catechesis from the angel (1:31–34), the Holy Spirit comes upon her (1:35a), and she receives the flesh of Christ (1:35b).

Mary is the mother of God and also the first catechumen. She sets the pattern for all who will follow her. "For nothing will be impossible with God" (v. 37). So Mary rejoices as the one favored by God to become the flesh-and-blood home of His incarnate Son. The Lord is with her indeed! By calling herself "the servant of the Lord" (v. 38), she humbly submits herself to God's word and to the miraculous presence with her and in her body. Mary serves as a model of the humble hearing of God's Word and the trusting response of faith created by that Word—the Word now made flesh in her womb.

Mary's Catechesis Is Catechesis for the Church

The Church celebrates the annunciation by the angel Gabriel to the Virgin Mary on March 25. In ancient times, March 25 was considered the first day of the new year, for many thought that on this day the creation of the world began. As early as the third century, many early Christian communities also thought that this was the day Christ was crucified, since it was possible for that first Good Friday to fall at the end of March. This united the creation and the redemption in the minds of the ancient Church. And it was not difficult for those early Christians to take the next logical step, that is, to suggest that Christ died on the same day of the month on which He was conceived. This is the reason many believe that Christmas is celebrated on December 25, nine months after the celebration of Jesus' conception and crucifixion.

Even though the early Christians had no solid evidence for all this, the theological consequences are intriguing. These early Christian communities believed that in the world's history there were four great days, all of which were on par with one another—the day God began to create the world, the day God came into this world, the day God offered Himself as the sacrifice for sins, and the day that God showed He was the final conqueror over sin, death, and the devil by rising from the tomb.

But what might Luke say about all this? He, too, describes the annunciation of the angel Gabriel to Mary as a day to be marked, a day that could be described as a festival of Christ, for on this day the old meets the new. All the promises of God in the Old Testament are now coming to fulfillment in Christ. Gabriel announces that the Messiah is coming, Jesus is the Lord, is the Son of the Most High, He is given the throne of His father David, He will reign over the house of Jacob, and of His kingdom there will be no end.

Why did He come? He was made in the likeness of sinful flesh in order to redeem sinful flesh. We who thought God was our enemy and our persecutor—we who lived in hostility to God as we wallowed in our fallenness—we poor sinners are the reason Jesus was conceived by the power of the Holy Spirit in the womb of the Virgin Mary, so His body, His flesh, could be offered up as an everlasting atonement and sacrifice for all sins. Jesus shared our common humanity in every way (except for sin); and because this child conceived in Mary is holy, the Son of God, He is able to redeem our bodies and make them holy like His body. And because His body rose from the dead, so also will our bodies rise in the resurrection of all flesh.

What a place to stand at the beginning of Advent! To stand in Nazareth with the Virgin and the angel Gabriel and look out across the life of our Lord to Jerusalem and to a cross and an empty tomb. What suffering and glory to behold! And to think that the baptismal waters that flow from His death and resurrection make us His holy children, in whom He dwells. And that the body and blood that flow from His sacrificial death are now received by us in, with, and under bread and wine for the forgiveness of all our sins, for our eternal benefit.

> And the angel answered her, "The Holy Spirit will come upon you, and the power of the Most High will overshadow you; therefore the child to be born will be called holy—the Son of God." . . . And Mary said, "Behold, I am the servant of the Lord; let it be to me according to Your word." And the angel departed from her. (Lk 1:35, 38)

Advent 2

Mary's Journey— The Visitation

Luke 1:39–45

Immediately upon hearing the announcement of the angel Gabriel and conceiving the Son of God in her womb by the power of the Holy Spirit, Mary journeys into the hill country of Judea to visit her cousin Elizabeth, who is in her sixth month of pregnancy. Mary's journey to Judea is the prelude to a series of pilgrimages. The culmination of these pilgrimages will be the journey of the Lord to a hill outside Jerusalem, where He will fulfill His earthly purpose.

But the purpose of Mary's journey is to visit her cousin Elizabeth, which brings John and Jesus together for the first time. What a mystery that their first meeting should come while they are still in the wombs of their mothers, who conceived these two children under such miraculous circumstances.

Mary's journey to visit Elizabeth has enormous significance for Luke's Jewish and Gentile readers! It shows them that Mary's womb is now the location of God's presence. This remarkable fact is demonstrated by an uncanny parallel between Mary's journey into the hill country and the movement of the ark of the covenant to the same locale on its way to Jerusalem (cf. 2 Samuel 6). Both the ark and Mary are greeted with shouts of joy; both are sources of elation for the households into which they enter; both David and Elizabeth are terrified at the presence of God's holiness; and both the ark and Mary stay in the hill country for three months. As a temporary and portable vessel housing the immanent presence of the true God, Mary appears to fulfill the purpose of the ark of the covenant.

Mary's Journey Creates a Response in the Creation

It is difficult for us to realize how earth-shattering the news of Mary's journey would be for Jewish persons reading these words twenty-five years after Jesus' ascension. They thought that God dwelled in the temple in Jerusalem, but now the evangelist is telling them that God was present in Mary. And, like the ark of the covenant, God journeyed throughout His land, visiting His chosen people with His presence.

Mary is the center of the visitation because Jesus, Son of Man and Son of God, is in her womb. But the action swirls around Elizabeth and her response to the presence of Mary and the baby in Mary's womb. What clearly stands out is the presence of God in the flesh in Mary and the reaction of Elizabeth and her unborn child to that presence. John leaps in his mother's womb because Jesus is there!

John, the forerunner, prepares the way of the Lord. The fleshly presence of the Messiah, the Creator, causes great things to take place within His creation, and this is the beginning. John's leap foreshadows the miracles of Jesus, who will cause all creation to shudder at His presence: "The blind receive their sight, the lame walk, lepers are cleansed, and the deaf hear, the dead are raised up, the poor have good news preached to them" (Lk 7:22).

The new creation comes to a people in the bondage of sin because Jesus, the Creator, has come in the flesh. Jesus stands in our place as the bearer of the bondage. Mary's unborn child will take upon Himself all sickness, demon possession, sin, and death as He journeys to Jerusalem in His final pilgrimage to the cross. There, in the darkness of Good Friday, all creation will shake and groan as He brings about the new creation through His suffering and death. When He cries, "It is finished," He proclaims that the new creation, begun with His conception by the Holy Spirit and announced by John when he leapt in Elizabeth's womb, is ended. And after a Sabbath rest in the tomb, Jesus rises on the third day declaring for all to hear that He has made all things new!

Mary's Journey Causes a Response of Song

Elizabeth sings the first hymn of the New Testament to Mary because Mary bears in her body the very Son of God: "Blessed are you among women, and blessed is the fruit of your womb!" (v. 42). Mary is blessed because God has visited her and she has responded in faith to God's promises. Elizabeth's hymn to Mary and the child in her womb is a response to the presence of God.

When the child in her womb miraculously leaps, Elizabeth, who is filled with the Holy Spirit (v. 41), interprets this as an expression of joy. Elizabeth is the first to worship the Christ Child; therefore, her words are the first Christian hymn. Jesus in the womb of Mary is proclaimed by Elizabeth to be Christ in His Church.

Ever since the time of Elizabeth's song to Mary, the Church imitates the worship of Jews by singing in the liturgy because God is present among us with His gifts! The Church always sings at celebrations, like weddings. The Church continually celebrates the presence of the Bridegroom in her midst as He comes to give her gifts. The Bridegroom comes to His Bride to teach her about the new creation and then celebrate the presence of this re-created world through the Meal of the new creation. Every time we gather to hear the Word of God and receive the Meal of God, God in Christ is bringing in His creation. What better reason to sing with Elizabeth, "Blessed are you among women, and blessed is the fruit of your womb!"

MARY'S JOURNEY IS A SIGN OF HER BLESSEDNESS

Mary's blessedness is an act of divine grace, which God gives to her as a gift. Mary is blessed because of the presence of Christ in her, just as the Church is blessed because Christ dwells in her. Mary's blessedness is a state of faith that grasps the promises of God that are coming to fulfillment in her. Mary is the vessel that contains the Son of God. Mary represents the Church not because of who she is, or even because of her faith, but because she bears in her womb the presence of Christ.

The Church is not the Church without the presence of Christ, and Mary would be just another pious Galilean woman if she had not been chosen to bear the Christ. Her body is the place where God resides for nine months. For the duration of her pregnancy, she becomes the tabernacle of God. The loins of Israel that carried the seed of the Messiah are now focused in the womb of Mary. The genealogies of Genesis have found their fulfillment. What other reason would prompt Elizabeth to proclaim: "Blessed are you among women, and blessed is the fruit of your womb"?

Mary is blessed among women because of what she now bears in her body for the life of the world. And she is blessed because of her faithful response to the angel: "Behold, I am the servant of the Lord; let it be to me according to Your word" (Lk 1:38). Mary receives the word of the angel in faith and submits to that word. Elizabeth now affirms what Mary said to the angel, namely, that Mary is the first among many who believe that God's promise to become flesh for our redemption was coming to fulfillment in the child in her womb.

MARY JOURNEYS
AS A FAITHFUL CATECHUMEN OF THE LORD

Mary is the first catechumen who received assurance from the word of catechesis from the angel Gabriel. She not only fulfilled Luke's stated purpose in writing the Gospel (1:4) but also pointed the way for Theophilus and all others who must confront the fleshly presence of God in the preaching and the Sacraments of the Church where God dwells and promises to be found.

Jesus will say, "My mother and My brothers are those who hear the word of God and do it" (Lk 8:21). Mary is the first to hear that word of promise and faithfully do it. And in response to the woman who cried to Jesus, "Blessed is the womb that bore You, and the breasts at which You nursed," a clear reference to Mary, Jesus corrects her by saying, "Blessed rather are those who hear the word of God and keep it!" (Lk 11:27–28). Mary, the mother of our Lord, heard the catechetical words of the angel, was anointed by the Holy Spirit, and conceived Jesus. She carried this holy Child for nine months in faith and raised Him as her Son in faith. She heard the word and then kept that word by living it out in faith.

As "hearers of the Word," we continue to receive in faith the gifts of life, salvation, and forgiveness that come from our Lord's catechesis. And this catechesis leads us down a narrow road to our own death and resurrection in the waters of Holy Baptism, and it continues as we enter His new temple to sit at table with Him along with Abraham, Isaac, Jacob, and all the saints. It is only as hearers of the Word that we learn what it means to be like Him—to forgive as He has forgiven us, to show mercy and compassion to a world that is hostile to us, and to do works of charity for those who need our help. As hearers of the Word, we continue to bring His gifts to the world by being "Christs" to our neighbor.

MARY'S JOURNEY WITH OUR SAVIOR

Mary's Son is our Savior. The fruit of her womb, which causes John to leap in Elizabeth's womb, confronts Israel with God's radical solution to our broken humanity. The visitation of Mary, pregnant with our Savior, to Elizabeth reminds us that through the Holy Ministry, Christ continues to visit and remain present among His people. As Mary carried the Savior within her, so the Church carries the presence of Christ in His Word and Sacraments, and wherever the Church carries His Word and Sacraments, there Christ is found. The same Christ who was conceived by the Holy Spirit and born of the Virgin Mary dwells among us here in the Gospel and the Sacraments. Our sanctuary is now like the hill country of Judea in that the same Jesus who dwelled there now dwells here. The same Jesus who was conceived in Mary's womb and who caused John to leap in Elizabeth's womb now dwells here with His gifts of grace. This Jesus, who walked the streets of Israel, bringing a new creation through His preaching and miracles, now resides among us, bringing the new creation through His teaching here in our Service of the Word and through this miraculous presence in, with, and under bread and wine.

MARY'S JOURNEY TO BETHLEHEM

Advent is our journey to Bethlehem, where we remember that our Lord was born in humility so that He might save us from our arrogance. As we journey with Mary and Joseph to Bethlehem, we contemplate our own journey—its joys and sorrows, its triumphs and tragedies. And no matter where our journey has brought us, we know that it began in Christ at the font where He joined Himself to us forever, that it continued with Christ as He nourished us along the way with the food of His Word and the food of His flesh, and that it will end with Christ as we await our blessed end, when we will join Him and all the saints in heavenly splendor.

But as we wait for Christmas and for His second coming, we join Elizabeth and all the saints, intoning that first hymn to Mary, the mother of God: "Blessed are you among women, and blessed is the fruit of your womb!" (1:42).

Advent 3

Mary's Song—The Magnificat

Luke 1:46–56

"The Magnificat is like an aria in opera; the action almost stops so that the situation may be savored more deeply."[3] After the dramatic relocation of the presence of God from the temple to the womb of the Virgin Mary, it should not surprise us that a well-developed liturgical chant should conclude this section on the birth announcements of John and Jesus. The Visitation marks the physical coming together of John and Jesus, but the Magnificat provides the theological significance of this meeting as Mary sums up her place in salvation history.

As our Advent preparations draw to a close, the mother of our Lord provides us with a magnificent hymn to summarize what mighty acts of salvation God is doing for us. It is a fitting conclusion to this season because it not only recalls for

---

3   R. Tannehill, *The Narrative Unity of Luke-Acts*, vol. 1 (Philadelphia: Fortress, 1986).

us who He is, but what we have become in Him. Mary's song is our song because it describes the Christian life as it is lived in Christ, in all its humility and all its sober splendor.

MARY'S HYMN OF PRAISE

Like any good hymn, Mary's Magnificat is poetic, shaped to be memorable for both the ancient and modern Church. This is why it is the normal canticle sung at Vespers and Evening Prayer (*LSB*, pp. 231–32, 248–49). The hymn is composed of two stanzas, the first one reflecting God's mighty acts upon Mary and her response of praise, the second one reflecting God's mighty deeds for Israel.

Echoes of Old Testament hymns are found throughout the Magnificat, especially in the use of parallel statements: "My soul magnifies the Lord, and my spirit rejoices in God my Savior" (vv. 46–47); "He has shown strength with His arm; He has scattered the proud in the thoughts of their hearts" (v. 51). Old Testament citations are sprinkled throughout, and a first-century Jew would hear an Old Testament hymn in Mary's song (cf. Hannah's song from 1 Samuel 2). (Different words for "magnifies" are used in our hymnals and Bible translations, such as "praises," "glorifies," or "proclaims.")

ACKNOWLEDGMENT OF GOD'S HOLY PRESENCE

Mary begins with two parallel acts of praise: she "magnifies the Lord" and she "rejoices in God my Savior." She concludes by saying that all generations will call her blessed (v. 48), because "He who is mighty has done great things" and "holy is His name" (v. 49). Curiously, none of these titles are the same as the titles in the annunciation except the final one: "holy." By describing God's name as "holy," Mary acknowledges that the child in her womb is the mighty God, who will accomplish the final acts of salvation.

God's holiness is accented for us to show us that our communion with Christ is the only thing that matters in this life, for it is with Him that we will dwell eternally. As we enter Christ's holy presence in the liturgy, we are entering the place where God wants us to be. In the worship service we receive a foretaste of our heavenly home.

GOD HAS REGARDED HER DESPITE HER LOW ESTATE

As the first Christian, Mary is struck with a desire to sing a hymn of praise. She believes these things will happen despite the lowliness of her condition because "He has looked on the humble estate of His servant" (1:48a). A similar expression is used by Elizabeth to describe how "the Lord has done for me in the days when He looked on me, to take away my reproach among people" (1:25). Luther stresses that God "looked on" this humble maid and downplays her "humble estate," for, in his words, "not her humility but God's regard is to be praised" (AE 21:314).

God looks with favor on those who are in physical distress, and every act of His mercy to individuals like Mary is simply a foretaste of God's restoration of Israel through the Messiah. By calling herself a "servant" (v. 48), Mary reminds us of her proclamation to the angel: "Behold, I am the servant of the Lord; let it be to me according to Your word" (1:38). God has chosen Mary to bear His Son precisely because of the lowliness of her condition!

God's regard for us is exactly like His regard for Mary. We bring nothing to God, and God does not regard us because of who we are or what we bring to Him. Our bondage to this fallen world is complete—we are helpless, impoverished, and destitute without God. For Him to regard us as servants is completely God's doing. We serve Him because His Word and Spirit have washed over us in holy water, because His Word enters our hardened ears and changes our vile bodies into holy ones as He dwells in us, and because His body and blood are tasted by us in bread and wine so that our flesh may be like His.

All generations will call Mary blessed because of the Child she bears in her womb. Mary is blessed because she is the mother of God, and God, "He who is mighty," has done great things for her. "He who is mighty" is the subject of the rest of the Magnificat. "He who is mighty" has done a mighty deed, scattered the proud, pulled down the mighty, exalted the humble, filled the hungry with good things, sent away the rich empty, and come to the aid of Israel (vv. 51–54). The "great things" refers to God's mighty acts of salvation, particularly the exodus and the Passover, His greatest acts of salvation in the Old Testament. God's final mighty act of salvation is the suffering, death, and resurrection of His Son, the child in Mary's womb. Mary exclaims here how she is blessed because God is using her to bring about His mighty acts of salvation.

God's Mighty Acts of Salvation for Israel

Lowliness is the theme of the second stanza of Mary's hymn, or what is sometimes called "the Great Reversal." Mary describes a world that is different from the normal expectations of human beings, where things are reversed, where the meek and humble, the poor and oppressed are blessed, and where the rich and powerful are "sent empty away" (v. 53).

"His mercy is for those who fear Him from generation to generation" (v. 50). Lowliness and reversal are accented by the emphasis on mercy that begins and ends this stanza. God has mercy for the generations of those who fear Him, and God remembers the mercy He continually offered to Israel's fathers, particularly Abraham, whose seed would produce Mary's child. Zechariah in his hymn at the birth of John will declare that the essence of God's action to save Israel is "to show the mercy promised to our fathers and to remember His holy covenant" (v. 72).

This mercy is the essence of Jesus' ministry. He comes as the merciful and compassionate Messiah and not as a God of vengeance. He does not punish His enemies for their sins against Him and others, but He places Himself under the Father's wrath, and He is punished as their substitute. This is how He shows mercy on the fallen creation—by releasing it from its bondage. He sets the captives free by releasing the demon-possessed, healing the sick, forgiving sinners, and raising the dead.

Mary's song shows how God's mercy has been shown to Israel. She describes the mighty arm of God scattering the proud and arrogant, a clear reference to the deliverance of the Israelites from the Egyptians. "He who is mighty" has repeatedly come to the aid of His servant Israel. God's mighty act of conceiving His Son in Mary's womb is to be placed in the context of God's mighty acts throughout the history of Israel.

But Mary also gives specifics on how this mercy expresses itself in the lives of the people of God and explains how God's principle of the "Great Reversal" works itself out. In God's kingdom, everything is the opposite of what you would expect: the first are last and the last are first, the humble are exalted and the exalted are humbled. As Luther says, "God is the kind of Lord who does nothing but exalt those of low degree and put down the mighty from their thrones, in short, break what is whole and make whole what is broken" (AE 21:299). God has brought down rulers from their thrones (Lk 1:52a) and has sent the rich away empty (1:53b). "To bring down" or "tear down" describes the action of removing the powerful from their positions of power.

All of us, no matter what our station in life, no matter how rich or poor we may be, act or think like the rich and powerful when we seek vengeance on our enemies. We might even ask God to help us in bringing about the demise of those who have used their power to hurt us. Such actions and thoughts show that we are part of this broken humanity that needs to be made whole by the Creator, who first made us in His image. God calls us not only to repent of our brokenness but also to confess our sins of hate and revenge.

Many in Israel thought the Messiah should come with power and might and punish those who had punished the righteous in Israel. Even John the Baptist, as he sat in prison, wondered if Jesus was failing as Messiah by not being a God of vengeance. But Jesus came not to inflict His wrath upon those who persecuted the faithful remnant, but to bring mercy on a creation that was in bondage to the root cause of all evil and hate. Jesus comes not to destroy but to re-create. He announces that the Father's wrath will not be poured out on His enemies but on His Son. This is the ultimate expression of God's mercy, the foundation for the mercy we now show to our enemies who hate and persecute us because we bear His name.

THE REVERSAL OF GOD'S SON

God's greatest act of salvation is the humble reversal of His Son. Jesus the Creator came to His creation as creature. As the Father exalted Jesus in His humility, so now Jesus will exalt those of humble origin. Simeon affirms this when he takes the 40-day-old Jesus and says that "this child is appointed for the fall and rising of many in Israel, and for a sign that is opposed" (2:34). And just before His death, Jesus predicts that God will show His glory through suffering when He cites Psalm 118 to the scribes and chief priests: "What then is this that is written: 'The stone that the builders rejected has become the cornerstone'? Everyone who falls on that stone will be broken to pieces, and when it falls on anyone, it will crush him" (Lk 20:17–18). As Luther says, "Christ was powerless on the cross; and yet there He performed His mightiest work and conquered sin, death, world, hell, devil, and all evil" (AE 21:340). Jesus, the humble child in the womb of this humble maidservant, shows God's hospitality to the world by coming to those who least expect it and bringing them salvation.

Mary's magnificent song reminds us that every song we now sing is a hymn that is inspired by the humble presence among us of the One who created us, the One who redeemed us, and the One who continually re-creates us by His Spirit and Word through simple water and simple bread and wine. Mary's song is our song because we may magnify the Lord only because Christ dwells in us and we dwell in Him. His humility is ours now, and as a result, His glory will be ours when we join Him and all the saints in heaven.

Mary's song ends on a simple note, "Mary remained with [Elizabeth] about three months and returned to her home" (1:56). Jesus, who caused John to jump in Elizabeth's womb, abides with His cousin and precursor through His mother, Mary. In this holy season of Advent, the Son of Mary abides among us and in us. With Mary we may now sing: "My soul magnifies the Lord."

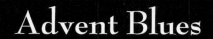

Advent Blues

Rev. Richard Andersen

The Church uses various colors to mark the different seasons of the Church Year. As we begin a new Church Year, we want to examine shades of the color blue, often used during Advent, to symbolize purity and royalty. Each sermon examines one of the roles of Christ: Christ as prophet, as priest, as king, and as Messiah.

Advent 1

Jesus as Prophet: Singing the Blues

Luke 7:16–17

I don't know much about music, but I know Webster's dictionary defines "the blues" as songs of "American Negro origin that are marked by the frequent occurrence of blue notes, and that take the basic form customarily improvised upon in performance of a 12-bar chorus consisting of a 3-line stanza with the second line repeating the first."[4] I know that because I looked it up. In essence, "the blues" refers to lyrics that are frequently sad. The sadness is often occasioned by love gone wrong.

There was something amiss in this world. The relationship between God and His people had somehow gone wrong. His creatures were singing "the blues." Sin had disrupted the relationship between the Creator and the created, but God heard the agonizing cry rising from the souls of His people. He responded. He sent His Son to articulate clearly to this troubled planet that God still loves His people and wants them to be one with Him. It is a timely message for us as well. The Savior came for us.

JESUS IS PREACHER

Jesus came to preach good news. While preaching this good news, our text records that He raised the lifeless form of a widow's only son from the dead. Those present praised God and said, "A great prophet has arisen among us!" (Lk 7:16). If, when that lad died, the widowed mother and her family had been plunged deep into "the blues"—into the depths of sadness—at the instant Jesus said, "Young man, I say to you, arise" (v. 14), they were no longer singing "the blues" but a jubilant chorale of praise and celebration!

William Barclay and other commentators have pointed out that Jesus considered Himself to be a preacher.[5] In fact, in Mark 1, Jesus tells His disciples that He must go on to the next town to preach "for that is why I came out" (Mk 1:38). His preaching was the means by which He fulfilled His primary mission that He described as "to

---

4   *Webster's Encyclopedic Unabridged Dictionary of the English Language* (New York: Gramercy, 1994), 162.

5   William Barclay, *The Mind of Jesus* (New York: Harper & Row, 1961), 131.

seek and to save the lost" (Lk 19:10). Paul said it clearly: "Christ Jesus came into the world to save sinners" (1 Tim 1:15). He came as the primary prophet of hope.

Threats were on the lips of other prophets. Jesus spoke of good news. Death no longer has dominion. Sin no longer is triumphant. Salvation is no longer elusive, but a gift given, a blessing bestowed, an honor offered to those who respond with faith.

Jesus Is Prophet

Whether on the mountain slopes of Galilee or the marble-pillared courtyards of Jerusalem's temple, Jesus came preaching and teaching. He also came as a prophet—not only to share the truth but also to be the truth. Thus He spoke in parables—simple stories that everyone, or at least most, could readily comprehend. He came healing the handicapped and helping the hungry. He made wine out of water and a feast for thousands out of a few fish and several loaves of bread. He calmed the stormy seas and enabled blind eyes to see. Nature acquiesced to His commands. Demons fled; lepers were cleansed. Shattered lives were made whole again because Jesus preached a love that chased away the blues, that turned hope into reality. He was and is a prophet who turns "blue" Mondays and other "blue" days of the week into days for merriment and celebration.

Although a prophet was also a preacher, some people today assume that Old Testament prophets only predicted the future. That was not all that prophets in the Bible did, of course, but certainly was a more sensational aspect of their work. Jesus, as that kind of prophet, is unexcelled, for who else foretold His own death, as well as His own resurrection? Who else announced the temple's destruction and advised His followers that the Holy Spirit would come lead them forth to evangelize the world? These and other truths were on the Lord's lips as He came to end the singing of spiritual "blues." Jesus, as prophet, came to color our world with joy, to change the hues of sadness to shades of cheer.

The Message Is Good News

Shusaku Endo, a famous Japanese Christian, has pointed out that John the Baptist delivered a "terrifying threat." This message revealed God's expectation of good fruit and His judgment against those who do not do so. But the proclamation of Jesus is the good news of the Gospel. Endo points out that "Gospel" means something joyful. Jesus' message did not make sinners afraid but was news of great joy.[6] Thus Jesus is the "ultimate prophet" because He reveals the truth of the Old Testament prophecies, bringing grace and life.[7]

---

6   Shusaku Endo, *A Life of Jesus*, trans. by Richard A. Schuchert (New York: Paulist Press, 1973), 45.

7   Lawrence O. Richards, ed., *The Revell Bible Dictionary* (Old Tappan, NJ: Revell, 1990), 828.

Jesus was different from the other prophets. He was different from Elijah and Elisha, Isaiah and Jeremiah, as well as His cousin John the Baptist, really the last of the Old Testament prophets. Jesus was different because of how He spoke. The other prophets spoke *for* God, but Jesus spoke *as* God. That is why He chases "the blues" so successfully.

At a performance of *Die Meistersinger von Nürnberg* by the Danish Royal Opera, the soprano lost her voice. She was able to act the role, though, so she moved her lips while a substitute sang the part from offstage. Even had they practiced the opera like that, they could not have performed better. They sang as one. Likewise, the prophets of old were spokesmen for God. As they opened their mouths, so the people heard the voice of God. They spoke as one. However, Jesus was like the other performers in the opera, those who sang their roles with their own voices.

Yet Jesus is more than they, for the singers memorized a libretto and a score by Richard Wagner, but Jesus composed His own lyrics—those that could only come from God Himself. Thus Jesus came as a prophet singing a song of good news to people who had long sung "the blues," but He did so not as an actor, but as the author—the one Peter called "the Author of life" (Acts 3:15).

This prophet comes to color your Advent season with love and forgiveness. Come, then, to the altar so that you may experience it all in wine and bread, Christ's body and blood, given and shed for you.

He comes to speak, to preach, to teach us that indeed "a great prophet has arisen among us!" And what good is that to us? In a time when sin is readily evident and guilt often traps us, we need to hear such a prophet. In an age that can become bleak with sad news emanating from the world's far corners, we must hear such good news. Listen, then, to Jesus, the Prophet, who seeks to paint our world with hope instead of dread, with joy despite sorrow. Permit Him to occupy the pulpit of your life daily to preach the good news so you no longer sing "the blues."

Advent 2

Jesus as Priest: Blue Ribbon

Hebrews 5:5–10

We are examining the Advent blues. Last week, we discovered we no longer need to sing "the blues," because Jesus, as prophet, preaches the Good News to dispel "blue" moods. Today we examine another of His roles: His role as priest. These are more than regal titles and lofty honors. They are claims Scripture makes for Jesus that Jesus Himself fulfills. Today, Jesus wins top honors with the blue ribbon.

Blue ribbons are commonplace for some people. A family I know has children who excel in everything they do. Their rooms are filled with trophies, plaques, and blue ribbons. The awards are for sports, academics, and music. Most of us are not so accomplished. We would be proud to have one blue ribbon. I don't even have one. I have won third place and honorable mention several times but never a blue ribbon.

It's impossible to list all the blue ribbons Jesus achieved, but Scripture boasts of at least one: "You are a priest forever, after the order of Melchizedek" (Heb 5:6).

MELCHIZEDEK—PRIEST AND KING

There could be no loftier award. Melchizedek was the most highly regarded priest of the Old Testament. He came long before Aaron, the high priest in the tabernacle. His family became the Levitical priesthood. Melchizedek was both priest and king of Salem, Jerusalem's old name. He was considered the "ideal ruler of Israel [in] later Jewish thought."[8] He met the founding father of Judaism, Abraham, with bread and wine following Abraham's rescue of his nephew Lot from the four kings (Gen 14:18–24). Psalm 110, which is messianic, affirms that Melchizedek was the most honorable priest known and that David's heir would be ordained by God to an eternal priesthood akin to Melchizedek (Ps 110:4). The writer to the Hebrews idealizes Melchizedek as the individual who joined the offices of king and priest. This blue ribbon of priesthood is the most distinctive kind—ancient and honorable—like the formal blue sash nobles wear to signify a high honor.

Yet for us today, some of this distinctiveness is lost by time. We cannot see how being compared to Melchizedek has importance. Therefore, it is essential to look

---

8   William P. Barker, *Everyone in the Bible* (Westwood, NJ: Revell, 1966), 235.

behind the words we read and to study their ancient origin. These words are critical; their imagery unparalleled; their truth unexcelled.

JESUS—HIGH PRIEST FOREVER

The writer to the Hebrews tells his readers that Jesus is not to be ignored as just another prophet, because He is truly a high priest of the loftiest kind. He notes Melchizedek was a "king of peace" (Heb 7:2). "Without father or mother or genealogy, having neither beginning of days nor end of life, but resembling the Son of God he continues a priest forever" (Heb 7:3). In short, Melchizedek is before the Aaronic priesthood was established in the days of Moses. His priestly authority is therefore timeless, and therefore Jesus' authority is likewise timeless. It is not constrained by Judaism. Not only did Abraham acknowledge Melchizedek as priest and king, but he paid him a tithe, which recognized his superiority as well. The Aaronic priesthood was ultimately set aside, but the priesthood of Melchizedek was established forever by his heir. That heir is Jesus. Jesus' priesthood is more than a blue ribbon—more, but at least a blue ribbon, because Jesus Christ is second to none.

Many of you may wonder why this is important. But in the earliest years of the Church, Jewish Christians were maligned for turning their backs on the Old Testament priesthood and the sacrificial system. Evidence of Jesus' priesthood was an important defense.[9]

JESUS IS SACRIFICE

The Epistle's author sees Jesus as both priest and sacrifice. According to Marcus Borg, the functions of the priest related to sin, sacrifice, and forgiveness provide for us the defining image of Jesus, our relationship through Him with God, and how we live our lives as Christians.[10]

But as Borg emphasizes, Jesus is not exclusively a priest, even a blue-ribbon one like Melchizedek. He is prophet, too, as well as king and Messiah. However, these titles should not limit us in our understanding of Jesus, because He is far more. Yet these roles enable us to see beyond the complexity of the Savior's personality, to see clearly the evidence that He is Lord of lords and King of kings, that he is more than another great teacher or another important philosopher. Jesus is God in His redemptive role as healer and guide.

That understanding, however, must stretch beyond the academic to reach the personal. While knowing Jesus as a blue-ribbon priest like Melchizedek is vital

---

9 Lawrence O. Richards, ed., *The Revell Bible Dictionary* (Old Tappan, NJ: Revell, 1990), 688.

10 Marcus J. Borg, *Meeting Jesus Again for the First Time* (San Francisco: Harper, 1994), 129.

knowledge, it is knowing Him personally, knowing His sacrifice, that makes Him a loving friend rather than an austere champion or celestial celebrity. Jesus is our priest, who ministers to us with His sacrifice, as well as His Sacraments. He ministers as a priest should to heal the body as well as the soul.

According to one Bible dictionary, in addition to teaching and offering sacrifices, priests diagnosed diseases that made worshipers ceremonially unclean and performed ritual purifications.[11] These were their primary roles. They are still the roles of Jesus, the priest, who wears the blue-ribbon honor of the "order of Melchizedek."

JESUS—GREAT PHYSICIAN

Jesus is our "great Physician" who heals us as did priests of old. Repeatedly, the evangelists tell us that countless people, infected with horrid and terrifying diseases, were brought to Jesus, who healed them. Not only the sick but also the dead were brought to Him. The blind saw; the dumb talked; lepers were cleansed. The bedridden walked. The hemorrhaging woman was cured. The mentally deranged were made sane.

But Jesus did not come to earth only to cure the sick; He came to bring the ultimate cure for our sin-sickness.[12] As a priest of the order of Melchizedek, Jesus could not ignore affliction in His people any more than He could ignore sin. The fact is: disease is the result of sin. It may or may not be *personal* sin that causes the disorder, but sin nevertheless, for sin is the instrument by which the devil seeks to divide us from God, to separate us from our Creator, and to claim us for his own. Jesus came for wholeness. He is not satisfied with shattered lives. He wants them to be complete. He preached not only to minds and hearts, but to the whole person—to ulcerated bodies, withered limbs, sickened organs, tainted minds, and sickly souls. His touch healed. His word cured. His ointments of saliva and dust were a prescription for wholeness.

In this age, we think of Jesus as Savior, but we forget that role is intended also to save us from sickness, which is the result of sin, as well as from Satan and evil's enigma. Thus let Jesus be your Melchizedek to bring you bread and wine as the original one did for Abraham, to forgive your sin so that you may experience healing of the body as well as healing of the soul and soundness of the mind. Holy Communion is a healing gift that Christ, our great High Priest, has given to us. Do not fail to celebrate it, not for the ceremony, the sip of wine and taste of bread, but for the assured forgiveness Jesus shares with His body and blood communicated in that gift. It is His way of making us whole with Him.

---

11 Richards, *Revell Bible Dictionary*, 816.

12 James S. Stewart, *The Life and Teaching of Jesus Christ* (Nashville: Abingdon), 85.

It is said that the British royal family was cruising on their yacht *Britannia* one night when the captain saw a bright, bluish light ahead in the mist. He sent an urgent message: "Please alter course!" The response was terse, "*You* alter course!" Angered by the arrogant response, he immediately responded, "This is John Jones, captain of the royal yacht. The Prince and Princess are on board. By the authority of the Queen, *you* change course!" The answer was instantaneous. "This is Fred Smith, keeper of this lighthouse for twenty-two years. *I can't change course!*"

Many of us want Jesus to sail different waters or to take another route to get out of our way. Then we discover that He is the lighthouse, "a priest forever, after the order of Melchizedek" (Heb 5:6), by whose light we must sail to be well forever, to be cured of our diseases, to be redeemed from our sin. We must change course and let Him guide us to safe harbor.

Advent 3

Jesus as King: Blue Blood

Luke 23:1–3; John 18:36–37

In our examination of Advent blues, we have been reminded that we no longer need to sing "the blues," because Jesus, as prophet, preaches the Good News to dispel "blue" moods. Also, we have been reminded that He has achieved the highest rank possible—the blue ribbon of the priest-king Melchizedek. These are more than regal titles and lofty honors. They are claims Scripture makes for Jesus that Jesus Himself fulfills. Today, we discover Jesus is a blue blood—descended from kings and a King in His own right.

Luke describes the scene before Pontius Pilate. Jesus was brought in by His accusers, who said, "We found this man misleading our nation and forbidding us to give tribute to Caesar, and saying that He Himself is Christ, a king." Then the Roman governor asked Jesus a salient question, "Are You the King of the Jews?" Jesus' response was simple. "You have said so" (Lk 23:2–3).

The evangelist John tells us a bit more. When Pilate asks Jesus what He has done to deserve the vengeance of the chief priests, Jesus answers: " 'My kingdom is not of this world. If My kingdom were of this world, My servants would have been fighting, that I might not be delivered over to the Jews. But My kingdom is not from the world.' Then Pilate said to Him, 'So You are a king?' Jesus answered, 'You say that I am a king' " (Jn 18:36–37).

The first time I saw a king and queen, I was in my thirties. I had lunch with Frederik IX and Queen Ingrid of Denmark at the Coconut Grove in the Los Angeles Ambassador Hotel. Of course, there were eight hundred other people there as well. Over twenty years later, I saw a second monarch, the United Kingdom's Queen Elizabeth II. Kings and queens don't often appear on the American landscape except as guests of state. Finally, last year I sat at dinner with Her Royal Highness, Princess Benedikte, sister of Queen Margrethe, when the American Club in Copenhagen observed its Diamond Jubilee.

To be sure, there are beauty queens and used car kings, monarchs of the movies and sovereigns of the playing fields, but they are not quite the same as true blue bloods. I have known any number of homecoming kings and queens, but I have known only one real, genuine, completely authentic King—not a pretender, not a king forced to abdicate, but a bona fide blue blood, the King of kings and the Lord of lords, Jesus.

JESUS IS OUR KING

You know Him too. He reigns from no golden throne and wears no diamond-encrusted crown. His kingdom is not one of boundaries and customs agents, but is, instead, of human hearts. His people are not those united by language or race or ethnicity, but by faith and prayer and the Sacraments—by God's Word and Christ's Church. His rule extends over the universe, but He has more than an embassy in every believing heart. He has a dwelling place, a palace of hope, a home where He Himself lives.

This is the one we know as Christ the King. This is the infant who drew Wise Men over the desert miles from the East, seeking the birthplace of history's most important King (Mt 2:1–12). This is the Rabbi whose teachings and miracles caused Galileans to try to take Him by force to name Him Israel's King (Jn 6:15). This is the one about whom the prophet Isaiah said, "He will reign on David's throne . . . forever" (Is 9:7 NIV). The prophet Micah foretold that He would be born in Bethlehem but would rule all Israel (Mic 5:2).

Jesus came to rule in the hearts of humankind. He came to advance the kingdom of God, which is the will of God. William Barclay identifies Jesus as the embodiment of the kingdom of God because He is the only one who has perfectly fulfilled the will of God.[13] Jesus came to be a far different King than earthly monarchs, a blue blood of heavenly blue.

He was born in no palace. His only crown was one of thorns. His only scepter was a reed. His regal cloak was a faded cape used in contemptible jest by His cap-

---

13 William Barclay, *The Mind of Jesus* (New York: Harper & Row, 1961), 54.

tors. He commanded no military force from the back of a stallion nor sentenced renegades to death from a judgment seat as did Pilate and Herod. But He touched the sick with healing hands and absolved the repentant from their awful deeds. Jesus was a King unlike any other. He was a King who died to save His people from their sins. Then He rose from the dead to rule with love and grace. He dispenses forgiveness rather than retribution, and welcomes everyone into His eternal kingdom. He was and is the most unpretentious blue blood this world will ever know.

BLUE-BLOODED FRIEND

Our King seeks to strengthen His rule in our lives so that when we fail, we repent. As we shed the sin and remember the lesson learned, we can move on with a new will to serve. "Be perfect," commands our King, "as your heavenly Father is perfect" (Mt 5:48). That is possible only as we allow King Jesus to erase sins and renew us with love's forgiveness. It is only when His blue blood courses in our veins that we are one with Him. It is only when King Jesus is not brushed off the throne of our hearts by a palace revolt that ignores Him, but when we willingly live as He lives, being faithful to Him despite our seeming faithless ways, that we discover we are freed, not condemned. We are loved, not loathed.

Oscar Wilde's *The Happy Prince* almost describes our King Jesus—regal blue blood, who is also a regular, ordinary friend. In the story, the people of the prince's kingdom, to remember this ruler who seemed always happy, erected a marvelous statue of him atop a tall column. They brightened it with gold leaf, used sapphires for its eyes, put a ruby in its sword, and decorated its neck chain with semiprecious stones and pearls. Whenever the people looked at the statue of the Happy Prince, they became happy too.

Late one fall, a swallow perched between the feet of the Happy Prince to spend the night. As he tucked his head under his wing, a large drop of water landed on the weary bird. He thought it strange that rain should fall on a cloudless, moonlit night. Looking up, he saw that the Happy Prince was not happy at all—he was crying.

The swallow flew to his shoulder. The prince told his new friend that though he was happy when he lived behind palace walls and never saw the condition of his people, now he could see the poor and the struggling, those enduring pain and those living with heartache. He asked the bird for a favor.

"Take the ruby from the hilt of my sword and carry it to that house some streets to the north, where a poor widow is caring for a sick child." The swallow obeyed. Entering an open window, he dropped the ruby where the mother would find it. Then the swallow cooled the air by flapping its wings, and the feverish child drifted off to sleep.

The swallow reported back to the Happy Prince, but the prince was still sad because there was another family about to be evicted from their home. "Take the jewels from my neck," instructed the prince, "and give them to the family." The swallow took the necklace, dropped it on the steps, and flew to a nearby branch to watch. When a child came out to look for twigs for the fire, he found the valuable jewelry and shouted with delight. The swallow reported back to the prince.

Days passed and the swallow needed to fly south, but there were other tasks his prince asked. The bird peeled off leaves of gold and dropped them in the cups of the beggars. Finally, the prince told him to take one of the sapphires from his eyes to help an orphan child who was selling matches. Then the Happy Prince asked the swallow to pry out the other sapphire and take it to a student's room. The student was destitute and so weak from hunger he could not study.

By now the swallow had delayed its flight south so long that it was too late to make the journey. He decided to stay and be eyes for the Happy Prince—to tell him about the happiness spread because of the prince's love for his people. The story continues in the same vein.

The Happy Prince is a legend, but the King of kings is a genuine blue blood who gave not jewels and leaves of gold to His subjects, but His life. He brought joy to our world not by offering glittering gems, but by giving us the sparkling gifts of salvation and love.

He came to be King of our hearts, so that we can love as He loves. He came to be King of our heads, so that we can think of others as He does. He came to be King of our souls, so that we can live as He lives—forever. He came to be King of our will, so that we can will what the Father wills—to do and be the truth.

Jesus is our joyous King, the happy Prince of Peace, who seeks to give us in bread and wine the living jewels of His body and blood. Come, then, and experience this King whose blue blood was so royal that it was shed for all His subjects to redeem them eternally. Come. The King awaits us. His Royal Highness, Jesus Christ, invites us to His feast of love.

Advent 4

Jesus as Messiah: Out of the Blue

Matthew 16:13–20

In our examination of Advent blues, we have been reminded that we no longer need sing "the blues," because Jesus, as prophet, preaches the Good News to dispel "blue" moods. Also, we have been reminded that He has achieved the highest honor possible—the blue ribbon of the priest-king Melchizedek. Last week we traced His life as King—a blue blood unlike any other. These are more than regal titles and lofty honors. They are claims Scripture makes for Jesus that Jesus Himself fulfills. Today, we discover Jesus as the Messiah, a gift "out of the blue."

A Gift "Out of the Blue"

Matthew's description of the event at Caesarea Philippi, late in the Lord's ministry, is familiar to most of us. Jesus was there with His twelve disciples, in a pagan place surrounded by statues of Greek and Roman gods and goddesses—particularly the god Pan. Jesus asks, "Who do people say that the Son of Man is?" The disciples responded with a variety of titles and names: "John the Baptist," "Elijah," "Jeremiah," and others.

"But who do you say that I am?" asks Jesus (Mt 16:13–15), seemingly out of the blue. Peter responds with his revealing answer, "You are the Christ, the Son of the Living God" (Mt 16:15–16). It was out of the blue that this understanding came, as did this Christ, this Messiah, this Promised One, this Anointed One of God. Jesus acknowledges that Simon Peter's revelation was given to Him by God: "Blessed are you, Simon Bar-Jonah! For flesh and blood has not revealed this to you, but My Father who is in heaven" (Mt 16:17).

But if it seems out of the blue—spontaneous, impulsive, and impetuous—it was not. John Stott says that Jesus "believed Old Testament Scripture to be His Father's revelation and that He was totally resolved to do His Father's will and finish His Father's work."[14] James Stewart points out that as Jesus interacted with and taught the disciples, these followers began to see Jesus' face "when they tried to think of God."[15] There was a gradual progression. It was not a hasty response. Jesus did not want His

---

14 John Stott, *The Cross of Christ* (Leicester: InterVarsity, 1987), 31.

15 James S. Stewart, *The Life and Teaching of Jesus Christ* (Nashville: Abingdon), 112–13.

role as Messiah to be a bolt out of the blue—an impromptu strike of lightning—but an executed plan that began with God and was carefully fulfilled in and through Jesus. How could people know Jesus as God's Son if He only trumpeted Himself? But by pointing to the Father, Jesus' followers saw that He was not just a son, but "the Son of the living God."

Jesus' Claim as Messiah

Yet Jesus' claim to the role of Messiah was not left only to His resurrection. At Caesarea Philippi, He acknowledged it to Peter and the rest of the disciples. After His arrest, when Jesus was asked, "Tell us if You are the Christ [the Messiah], the Son of God," He answered, "You have said so" (Mt 26:63). Mark quotes Jesus saying directly, "I am" (Mk 14:62). In His last days, Jesus was not hesitant to claim His messianic role, but primarily He was determined to be the Messiah for whom the Jews hoped.

Because of ancient prophecies, the Jews looked forward to when the Messiah would come. Daniel and Isaiah painted wondrous pictures of Him. But "about 70 B.C. there emerged a book which spoke much about the Son of Man, and which sharpened and intensified the picture," writes William Barclay.[16] The Book of Enoch proclaimed the Messiah to be militant. Terror would grip His enemies. In this book, the Messiah is "a divine, superhuman, apocalyptic figure." He will destroy God's enemies and lift up the righteous.[17] This was not the Messiah Jesus came to be, thus He had to teach people all over again that the views of Daniel and Isaiah's Suffering Servant were accurate. Enoch's view was patriotic, comforting to the beleaguered Jews, but its suggestions were romanticized nationalism.

To John the Baptist's inquiry if He was the Messiah, Jesus responded, "Go and tell John what you hear and see: the blind receive their sight and the lame walk, lepers are cleansed and the deaf hear, and the dead are raised up, and the poor have good news preached to them. And blessed is the one who is not offended by Me" (Mt 11:4–6). At Nazareth, when He preached in His own synagogue, Jesus read the words of Isaiah: "The Spirit of the Lord is upon Me, because He has anointed me to proclaim good news to the poor. He has sent Me to proclaim liberty to the captives and recovering of sight to the blind, to set at liberty those who are oppressed, to proclaim the year of the Lord's favor" (Lk 4:18–19). When He finished, Jesus said, "Today this Scripture has been fulfilled in your hearing" (Lk 4:21). Here is the Messiah God designed, and Jesus fulfilled—out of the blue. He was not a national rescuer, but an international, multicultural, multiracial Savior.

---

16 William Barclay, *The Mind of Jesus* (New York: Harper & Row, 1976), 145.

17 Barclay, *Mind of Jesus*, 146.

THE MESSIAH SAVES

As the Prophet above all prophets, the Priest unexcelled, the King who reigns above all kings, Jesus is the Christ, the Messiah, the one who comes in love. St. Paul says that through Him, God reconciled to Himself all things "making peace by the blood of His cross" (Col 1:20). Paul wrote to the Romans, "But God shows His love for us in that while we were still sinners, Christ died for us" (5:8).

In the South Pacific during World War II, a nineteenth-century Melanesian religion was revived among tribal peoples. Airplanes dropped immense crates of supplies to help the embattled people with food and medicines and also dropped weapons and war equipment for the armies defending them. As the people were primitive, they thought it was one of their gods blessing them with material gifts dropped out of the blue. Thus the cult became a thriving religion.

The plan of salvation was not intended to provide material wealth or war supplies, but eternal joy. Jesus the Messiah was not an impromptu supply drop, but One whose planned invasion of earth had been carefully charted by heaven long ago. Thus the prophets foretold Him. A people was appointed to receive Him. And God gave to the world, out of the blue, a promise long made and now fulfilled. It was Jesus, the infant of Bethlehem. It was Jesus, the carpenter of Nazareth. It was Jesus, the Galilean rabbi. It was Jesus, the crucified one of Calvary, and the risen one of Easter. In Him all the pieces of the puzzle of salvation fit together—all the prophecies and all the proofs of His earthly ministry. Jesus came from out of the blue, intent on fulfilling the Father's plan to save the world. It was not a momentary decision but the plan that love carved out before the beginnings of the universe.

Jesus is Messiah. Alleluia! Prophet, Priest, and King, the Christ of God. Alleluia!

Christmas Eve

Baby Blue and Royal Purple

Matthew 1:18–25

It was a boy Mary would bear. It was a royal baby, heir of David, the king!

Baby blue and royal purple would be the natural choice of colors if we were to decorate His nursery properly! But alas, there was no nursery. There was a stable, perhaps only a stable in a cave. "Rude and bare" was His manger, as the carol says ("As with Gladness Men of Old," *LSB* 397:3). There were no trappings, no tapestries, no garlands, no ribbons, no robes, and no festooned draperies of baby blue and royal purple—only the smoke-blackened walls of a cave and a well-used feedbox. Nothing more.

A REGAL SETTING

Yet in the simplicity of Jesus' nativity we have something more regal than any palace could provide. It is not the setting that gives Jesus His noble titles, King of kings and Lord of lords, but God Himself. It is not the colors baby blue and royal purple that matter, but the pitch-black sins and blood-red offenses of His people that Jesus came to erase. The colors for salvation's joy are the hues of Noah's rainbow sprinkled with the diamond dust of a starlit night, the gold of angelic heralds, and the silver of their sparkling news.

Matthew states clearly that Jesus is not just another baby born in the squalor of the times. He describes the birth of the Messiah, the long-awaited chosen one of God, the one whom prophets had foretold, and the one apostles would proclaim.

It is no ordinary birth. Jesus was not conceived as other children. "She was found to be with child from the Holy Spirit," Matthew explains (1:18). Later he assures us that Joseph took Mary as his wife, "but knew her not until she had given birth to a son" (v. 25). It was a miraculous event unlike any other. This marvelous incarnation was God's use of nature as well as a glorious demonstration of His supreme authority over nature. It was no magical act, astonishing, but deceptive. It was God entering into the human world to experience it in human form.

So the King came as a baby. His kingdom was not of this world, but His infancy most certainly was! He was nursed and nurtured, caressed and cradled. He hungered and cried as an infant. He needed His clothes changed. He grew weary; He slept. We can imagine that He smiled at the worn faces of shepherds and laughed at the dark beards of the Magi. He gave up his equality with God. Paul writes, "But made Himself nothing, taking the form of a servant, being born in the likeness of men. And being found in human form, He humbled Himself by becoming obedient to the point of death, even death on a cross" (Phil 2:7–8).

BLUE TO RED

Jesus, the wondrous Babe of Bethlehem, came to die the death of a sacrificial lamb. He came to make a conquest of life and death with new life. His colors would not always be baby blue or even royal purple. The red blood of the cross would change these colors to the majestic hues of heaven. Jesus came to offer our world hope and peace. Jesus came so that our lives would be less "blue" and more royal.

When Danish Queen Margrethe II visited a home for the elderly, it had been announced in advance and everyone knew she was coming. They recognized her immediately, except for one elderly, nearly deaf woman who kept asking who came in with all the fanfare. She couldn't hear the answers, so even as the Queen shook her hand, the woman was still asking those around her who had come. "Dronningen," the Queen whispered. The woman did not understand. Again the Queen said in Danish, "The Queen." Still, the woman was puzzled. When the Queen realized the woman was deaf, she almost shouted, "The Queen!" Then the woman not only heard, but also recognized the Danish monarch standing before her. Embarrassed, she asked why someone hadn't told her earlier. Her cohorts laughed.

It was no laughing matter when Jesus appeared and was not recognized. The world turned a deaf ear to the "baby blue" infant of Bethlehem, just as later it plugged its ears to the "royal purple" Good News with the din of legalism and denial. But fortunately, God keeps shouting for us to recognize Him, to hear that the King has come and His name is Jesus, Immanuel, "God with us." He keeps shouting that He loves us and seeks our membership in His royal family.

This Christmas we remember baby blue and royal purple are merely color swatches in time. Jesus grew from infancy to manhood, and from manhood to Saviorhood. He grew beyond the shades of human coloring to be the vivid Lord of all. From cradle to cross, from Bethlehem's cave to Calvary's crucifixion, Jesus painted an image of God's immense love for us. As Easter dawned and the conquest of death became complete, we thrilled to the golden sunrise that changed the color of life forever. Instead of dull and depressing, His victory gave life the brilliance of joy. If no longer baby blue, He has nevertheless shared with us the purple of the palace of eternity and made us through Baptism His brothers and sisters forever.

As we savor the goodness of His love in a simple wafer of bread and sip of wine, we recognize that Jesus imbues our lives with more than color—He offers forgiveness and love that never blur or fade or wash out.

Let us, then, like the shepherds, savor the miracle of Christmas and experience the baby blue of God's grace and the royal purple of His salvation.

The Gospel in a Nutshell

Rev. Herbert E. Hoefer

Each of these Advent midweek sermons is based on one phrase of John 3:16.

Advent 1

God Loves Us

John 3:16

At home it's a bit of a joke as to when I'm going to preach my "anti-Christmas sermon" each year. This year, this is it. I've chosen Jn 3:16 as the text for my Advent sermons this year. The verse has often been called the Gospel in a nutshell: "For God so loved the world, that He gave His only Son, that whoever believes in Him should not perish but have eternal life."

I'd like to begin with the first word in the verse: *God*. "God so loved." You wouldn't think "God" would need much emphasizing. It should be rather obvious. But if you asked anyone what this Christmas season is about spiritually, what responses would you get? Christmas? It's about love. It's about caring for the needy. It's about peace on earth. It's about goodwill among people. And we haven't even come to Santa Claus and presents and cookies and family time and so forth.

CHRISTMAS IS ABOUT US

Think about that list—there's nothing wrong with it, especially the cookies. But it's all about us. It's about what we do, what we desire. We could call these holidays our annual winter frolics and it would be the same thing. There is some good in what we do and what we desire. We recommit ourselves to each other. We give to the needy. We talk about love and goodwill and peace and family. We know we cannot survive as a community without these goals, so there is a reason to have an annual festival or recommitment.

It's good and necessary, but it ignores God. We praise ourselves, not Him. We admire how good we are, what good things we do, what love and commitment we show. We are proud of our community. We feel good about ourselves.

We can do some good things. Anyone can—whether Hindu or Muslim or atheist. We all have "the work of the law . . . written on [our] hearts" and our "conscience also bears witness" (Rom 2:15). That's not peculiarly Christian. That's true in every society and every religion. They all teach love and goodwill and peace and unity.

No society can exist without these teachings, and every society has an annual celebration emphasizing them. Typically that festival comes at the end of the community's calendar year—often at the winter solstice when the sun reaches its lowest point in the sky and the new cycle of nature begins. But this is social goodness. This is social survival. This is religion in the service of community goodwill. There is nothing wrong with it, but it is not Christmas. It is not Christian. It is not godly.

IS IT IDOLATRY?

In fact, it can easily become idolatry. We make ourselves into gods. We praise ourselves: "Look at what a good boy I am." We set up standards of goodness, meet them, and admire ourselves: "Who needs forgiveness when you love and give and care so generously as I do each Christmas?" We create our own religion of good works. We create our own standards of righteousness. We create our own god and—wonder of wonders—he looks just like us!

We hear moving stories about wars stopping at the front lines on Christmas Eve. One side sings "Silent Night" in their language, and the other joins in theirs. Soldiers even leave their trenches, shake hands, and treat each other as fellow humans. They congratulate themselves on their goodness. But what happens the next day? Does peace prevail? No, it's built on sand. It's built on the illusion of our wonderful human goodness.

Only God's goodness is real. The message of Scripture is that you and I are not the source of goodness. The word *God* means "good." As James tells us, "Every good gift and every perfect gift is from above, coming down from the Father of lights" (James 1:17).

What is goodness? The goodness you and I experience is the sin-ridden goodness of our fallen world. True goodness is only in God. Scripture tells of God's ability to forgive—time and time again. "For My thoughts are not your thoughts, neither are your ways My ways, declares the LORD" (Is 55:8; cf. v. 9; Ps 103:11; Rom 11:33). "I am God and not a man" (Hos 11:9). "If we are faithless, He remains faithful—for He cannot deny Himself" (2 Tim 2:13).

This is our source of comfort and confidence in life and in death. God not only forgives, but He also forgets. He completely wipes our slate clean because of Christ. "I will forgive their iniquity, and I will remember their sin no more" (Jer 31:34). When we humble ourselves before Him and pour out our hearts, He takes our sin and weakness and rebellion and swallows it up. It's gone—forever. That's goodness. That's love. That's divine. That's the goodness of Christmas. "God so loved."

LOVED THE WORLD

It is significant that John says God so loved the world. The world in John's Gospel is the enemy of God. It's the world that won't recognize and receive Him (Jn 1:10–11). It's the world that will hate us, His followers (Jn 15:18). It's in the world that we will have tribulation (Jn 16:33). Satan is "the ruler of this world" (Jn 12:31).

Yet, in John's Gospel, Jesus is "the Savior of the world" (Jn 4:42). He "takes away the sin of the world" (Jn 1:29). He is "the light of the world" (Jn 8:12). And in this Christmas text, "God so loved the world." What a tremendous comfort that is—because the world is me. I often don't recognize and receive Him. I often rebel against Him. I often let Satan control the direction and priorities of my life. The holy, righteous God of the universe, the Creator of all things (including me), the Judge of all eternity should be revolted by the world in me. He should condemn and reject and punish the world and me.

He should, and did. He did that in Christ. Christ, the unblemished Lamb of God, gave His life like the lamb at Passover so that the angel of death would pass over. God's righteous judgment and wrath had to be exacted. Instead of falling on me, it fell on Jesus. He was consumed in God's holy wrath so I can stand free and forgiven and righteous before God—purely by grace.

God is not like us. God is good. He does not love as we do. He does not forgive as we do. His ways are not our ways. As far as the heavens are above the earth, so far surpassing is His love beyond ours (cf. Ps 103:10–11).

WE LOVE HIM

And we love Him. We see ourselves as His dearly beloved children. We pray to Him, trust Him, and seek to serve Him. And we fail. We fall back into old habits. We are ashamed to speak up for Him, even in this season of His birth. We spend money on dozens of useless things but give so little to Him. We give a pittance to the poor and the needy, then pat ourselves on the back. And what does God say? He says, "I love you." That's incomprehensible. That's unreasonable. That's unimaginable. That's superhuman. That's goodness. That's God. "God so loved the world."

When we see the Christ Child this Christmas, let's think of that. He came to the world weak and alone and one with us. It was true then, and it is true now. The Christ Child is born in us today, in our world, in our failure and rebellion and weakness.

He is born in us at His Table. He comes in His very body and blood and lives anew in us, in our fallen world. Although we abuse Him, though we let Him down, though we fail Him, though we resent Him, though we hurt Him, He comes. He welcomes us to His Table. He asks only that we welcome Him.

Advent 2

God Keeps His Promises

John 3:16

The Old Testament was a time of prophets and promise. It was the time of waiting or anticipating—and then it happened. God sent "His only Son." The New Testament is the time of celebrating the promise fulfilled.

The Advent season focuses on the coming of that Messiah. We are invited to enter into the Old Testament experience, to yearn and hope and wait. Just as children wait weeks in expectation before they are allowed to open presents, so we are invited during these weeks of Advent to enter that spirit of painful expectation spiritually. In some churches, Christmas carols are not sung during the Advent period of waiting.

WAIT FOR THE SURPRISE

If we can sense the pain and frustration of the Old Testament peoples, we can better rejoice at the fulfillment. When the angels finally announce, "Unto you is born this day in the city of David a Savior, who is Christ the Lord" (Lk 2:14), we can rejoice just as those first shepherds did. If we don't feel the pain, we won't feel the joy. If we don't wait, we won't really celebrate.

Sometimes all we have in life is the promise as in that well-known adage: "Faith is only faith when you have nothing else to hold on to." The Old Testament prophets didn't know what to expect. They knew it would be "a righteous Branch" sprung from the stump of David's house (Jer 23:5). "The days are coming, declares the LORD, when I will fulfill the promise I made to the house of Israel" (Jer 33:14).

The prophets did not know the Messiah would be God Himself. They had no concept of Father, Son, and Holy Spirit, so they couldn't possibly anticipate that the Second Person of the Trinity would be born as man, that the Father would send "His only Son."

They knew He would "[exercise] steadfast love, justice, and righteousness in the earth" (Jer 9:24), but how could they know that it would be a righteousness rooted in the forgiveness of sins, won on a cross? They thought it would be justice and righteousness for their nation. How could they anticipate that it would be for all people and for all eternity? Sometimes all we have in life is the promise, and we just wait. We wait and God surprises.

Waiting Hurts

It's hard to wait. We heard the psalmist say, "Out of the depths I cry to You, O Lord! O Lord, hear my voice! . . . I wait for the Lord, my soul waits, and in His word I hope" (Ps 130:1–2, 5). Sometimes all we have in life is the promise, and it hurts.

Can you think back to times in your life when all you had was the promise? Do you remember times when you were in the depths and cried to the Lord, and all you could do was wait? Those were painful times. Do you recall the loneliness? the frustration? the anger? the doubt? Maybe you even felt guilty that you had those feelings. How can God love me when I feel like this? No wonder He's left me like this.

Maybe you're going through a painful experience now. Maybe you go through it every Christmas season. This season can bring to the surface all the frustrations and losses and fears of life. For many, these weeks before Christmas are the most painful days of the year. They can't wait for Christmas to be over. Many people wear a mask of "good cheer," but inside they feel only pain and hurt and frustration. Outside it's "Merry Christmas! Oh yes, the singing and bells are wonderful!" Inside it's "I don't have the perfect life everybody else has. I can act it, but I'll never have it. I don't want to spoil it for you. I'll never tell you what I'm really feeling."

And so it goes on year after year. Will the pain ever end? Will Christmas ever pass? "What is wrong with me that I can't be happy like everyone else?" Christmas is the time of greatest depression, loneliness, and suicide in our society.

God Sends His Son

Sometimes all we have in life is promise, and we wait. But we have a promise that comes from God Himself. And He is the God who fulfills His promises. That's precisely what we celebrate. "When the fullness of time had come, God sent forth His Son, born of woman," Paul wrote (Gal 4:4).

There is a "fullness of time" also in your life. Think back. Remember those times of pain and frustration and doubt? Remember how your good Lord saw you though that? Most likely He didn't lead you out as you anticipated, but He did lead you out—"in the fullness of time," when it was right, when you were ready, He sent His Son.

He did it in Jesus. He did it in your life. He's doing it now. That's the story of our life in God. It's a life of trust. It's a "turning over" of our fears and worries and burdens. It's a freedom of knowing He's in charge, a confidence that He will act. Our whole Christian life is waiting on Him. It's trusting Him—His love, His will, His goodness.

Can we stop and look behind the mask of the hurting people around us? Can we see their special pain this time of year? Can we hold their hand in God's name and help them hang on and wait? Tell them the great Christmas truth: God kept His promise from the Old Testament and sent His Son. God keeps His promises to all who wait on Him—in the fullness of time, in the most unexpected ways, He still sends His Son.

Advent 3

God Makes His Will Our Will

John 3:16

"Whoever believes in Him should not perish." God makes His will our will. That is God's will for us, for everyone. God's will is for "all people to be saved and to come to the knowledge of the truth" (1 Tim 2:4). That is why He gave His one and only Son that we may believe and not perish. That is the prayer our Lord Jesus prays for us every day, even now at the right hand of the Father: "[Father,] I do not ask that you take them out of the world, but that you keep them from the evil one" (Jn 17:15).

We know what God's will is. We know what Jesus' prayer is. The question is what *our* will is, what *our* prayer is. Is our will that we believe in Him? Is our prayer that we not perish? Is that our prayer for our loved ones and family and friends? As we know and hear so often during this season, commercialization has taken over Christmas. Our sight has been directed toward things instead of toward Him. Our thoughts are on presents and arrangements and parties instead of on Him.

WHAT IS OUR WILL?

What is our will this time of year? Do we want the perfect gift for each person on our list—without maxing out our credit card in the process? What is our prayer? Do we plead to get everything in place in time? What is our prayer for our loved ones and family and friends? Do we hope they cooperate and not get in each other's hair?

The last thing we think about is whether we "believe in Him" or if our friends are "perishing." And yet, in the midst of the season's mindless revelry, what would happen if we kept a spirit of Advent? What if we thought of "preparation" and "repentance" before attending the office or neighborhood or family Christmas party? What if we read the text we just heard from Rom 13:12–14? It advises us to "cast off the works of darkness and put on the armor of light," to "walk properly as in the daytime, not in orgies and drunkenness, not in sexual immorality and sensuality, not in quarreling and jealousy." Instead, it recommends we "put on the Lord Jesus Christ, and make no provision for the flesh, to gratify its desires."

What if we truly did clothe ourselves with the Lord Jesus Christ before we went to that party? What would this Christ-wearing man see? What would this Christ-wearing man say? How would he act? Should he participate? Would he object? If we truly did clothe ourselves with the Lord Jesus Christ, would we confront? Would we walk out? Would we be offended? If we put on Christ, had Him as close as a second skin, what would Christ think of where we took Him, what we thought, what we said, and what we did?

What Are Our Priorities?

Christmas shows us clearly what our priorities are. We try to justify them. We say everyone does it. We say this is what people expect. We say a person has to have family and friends. Christmas reveals to us what is important in our lives and what we are willing to compromise and whom we are willing to offend—our Lord or our friends? Would we max out our credit card on a gift to the Lord?

And so the faint voice of our Lord's call comes through the din of Christmas sounds, "Believe in Me and pray, lest you perish. Pray for others, lest they, too, perish." Advent is a time to prepare our hearts. It is a time to reflect and repent. We realize who and what we really are. We say with David in Psalm 51:

> Have mercy on me, O God, according to Your steadfast love. . . . Wash me thoroughly from my iniquity, and cleanse me from my sin! . . . You may be justified in Your words and blameless in Your judgment. . . . Purge me with hyssop, and I shall be clean; wash me, and I shall be whiter than snow. . . . Then I will teach transgressors Your ways, and sinners will return to You. (Ps 51:1–2, 4, 7, 13)

Can you imagine what would happen if you came to a Christmas party with that mentality? I will be a repentant, forgiven sinner here. I will not condone their ways by my silence. I will be a presence of Jesus Christ here. I will teach transgressors Jesus' ways so they will come unto Him. How would you do that? How would you act when things got out of control, turning into the "loose living and drunkenness and reveling" that God despises? Can you in good conscience participate? Do you make a scene?

REPENT AND PREPARE

What do we do when God's will is ignored and flaunted? Do we separate ourselves so that we also do not perish and get drawn into it all? How do we "believe in Him" and still live in the world—especially at Christmas?

We repent and we prepare. We "cast off the works of darkness" in our own life and "put on the armor of light" (Rom 13:12). I don't have the simple answer for your life or for mine. But I do know what God's will is, just as you do. As James writes, it is "to keep oneself unstained from the world" (James 1:27).

How that battle will take place in your life, I don't know. But I do know we need to prepare for it. It will arrive. Perhaps we went along with the flow before, but this time it will be different.

We will fail, time and time again. But we will not be the same. This will not be just another Christmas. The parties will not be just uncomfortable bashes. Those spending sprees will not be unquestioned. We will be forgiven sinners and will show it. Others will know it, and we will pray that they believe in Him and not perish.

Advent 4

God Gives Eternal Life

John 3:16

We have come to our last Advent sermon on the Gospel in a nutshell, John 3:16: "God so loved the world, that He gave His only Son, that whoever believes in Him should not perish but have eternal life."

The point of Christmas, the purpose of God, is that we have everlasting life. When Eve and Adam sinned in the Garden of Eden, they were immediately sent out: "Lest he reach out his hand and take also of the tree of life and eat, and live forever" (Gen 3:22). If they had taken fruit from that tree also, they would never die. Only if they died would they be free from their sinful nature and this fallen world. Only if they died could they enter everlasting life. Only then would there be mourning and suffering no more and every tear be wiped from their eyes forever (Rev 21:4).

A Christmas Without . . .

Often our sights are lowered during Christmas celebrations. We are urged to look at the good things of life: good cheer, good family times, good presents, goodwill among people. These things certainly are good, but they are not the point of Christmas. This is not why Jesus came. "God so loved the world, that He gave His only Son, that whoever believes in Him should not perish but have eternal life"—not better temporal life.

Can we have a Christmas celebration without good cheer, good family, good presents, goodwill? Can we enjoy Christmas without these temporal blessings? Can we rejoice with great joy when we have nothing to be cheery about—no family around us, no presents, strife and jealousy and vindictiveness? For many in our society this is the Christmas they have, the life they have. Can they rejoice?

In some ways, they can rejoice better than those of us blessed with good cheer, good family, good presents, and goodwill. They have a better chance to find the true joy and meaning of Christmas. This joy and meaning are not found in good cheer, in family, in presents, in goodwill; they are found in God—in His love and promises. "God so loved the world."

It is the goodness of God, not the goodness of life or of people or of family, that we celebrate. It is on His goodness that we build our lives. His goodness, brought to us in Christ, assures everlasting life to all who believe in Him.

Where are our sights set this holiday season? What will determine if it is a joyful Christmas? What if family plans and gift-giving and partying completely fall apart? What if, in the words of Luther's hymn "A Mighty Fortress Is Our God," "take they our life, goods, fame, child, and wife" (*LSB* 656:4)? Would we still be able to celebrate Christmas? What is the point of the celebration? Who is the point of the celebration? What blessing does Christmas promise? Is there a reason to "Sing aloud and shout, to rejoice and exult with all your heart," no matter what Christmas is like in our life?

Christmas Is Invasion

Christmas is the great rescue event of God. We were captive to "the ruler of this world" (Jn 12:31). We were in bondage to sin, lost in our trespasses and sin. We were doomed to God's just wrath and punishment of our sins. We were rightly destined to hell. We belonged to Satan and his kingdom forever.

And then came the invasion. In "the fullness of time," when the conditions were right, God made His assault on Satan's kingdom. It was simple but clear. It was the Second Person of the Trinity, born of Mary as Jesus of Nazareth in the little town of Bethlehem. Satan tried vigorously to thwart the attack. He moved King Herod to snuff out the young life. God countered by warning the Magi to return home by a different route. God warned them not to tell Herod where the child was. Satan countered by having Herod kill all the babies in the region of Bethlehem. God countered by warning Joseph in a dream to move Jesus and Mary to Egypt until Satan's henchman, Herod, died.

Satan unsuccessfully tempted Jesus in the wilderness as Jesus began His frontal attack at age 30. Satan then left Him "until an opportune time" (Lk 4:13). Jesus drove out the demons and asserted His power over Satan's armies. He healed and raised the dead and called people to join His victorious ranks. Finally, Armageddon arrived, a Waterloo battle climaxed on Mount Calvary. The Father released Satan to inflict the tortures of hell upon His one and only Son. Jesus was abandoned by God for three hellish hours on the cross and Jesus screamed, "My God, My God, why have You forsaken Me?" (Mk 15:34).

Why? So that you and I may never undergo that hell, the hell we deserve. He took your place and mine. He was the spotless Lamb of God who takes away the sin of the world, your sin and mine. He won the battle against Satan, "becoming obedient to the point of death, even death on a cross. Therefore God has highly exalted Him and bestowed on Him the name that is above every name, so that at the name of Jesus every knee should bow, in heaven and on earth and under the earth, and every tongue confess that Jesus Christ is Lord, to the glory of God the Father" (Phil 2:8–11).

That's what Christmas is. Do we believe that? Do we celebrate that? Do we accept that gift of eternal life? Christmas is the D-Day invasion, the day our liberation began. That is something to hold our focus. That is reason to rejoice. That is *the* reason to rejoice.

Angles on Advent Angels

Rev. Timothy P. Wesemann

Advent 1

Joseph's Angle

Matthew 1:18–25

What's your angle on angels? You must have one. Angels are everywhere. Literally, they are all around us—the ones we can't see and the ones we do see. God's angels fill the heavens and earth, worshiping and serving Him, while also serving and protecting us by God's command. God's Word also describes them as messengers. But there are other angels around us. They are humanity's angelic creations, the ones we hang on our walls, portray in pictures, or place on our Christmas trees. There are angel magnets, pins, and stained glass. In some places entire stores are dedicated to the sale of angel paraphernalia.

So what's your angle on angels? Are they part of your daily life, or do you rarely think about their role? Do you have a "cute" angle on angels, thinking of them as adorable charms made for collecting? Or do you often consider the ongoing battles angels fight against the spiritual forces of evil in the heavenly realms on your behalf? Most of us have an opinion, or angle, on angels. In this Advent series, we prayerfully consider how God used angels to prepare the world for its Savior, Jesus, the Christ.

Most of us have been in situations where we pace the floor, praying for an answer. We feel anxiety mixed with anger and confusion. Sleep seems out of the question. There is an inner wrestling, a continual struggle. What's the right decision? We cling to the hope that God will disclose the perfect solution, His perfect resolution to the problem.

JOSEPH HAD A PROBLEM

Joseph felt this same consternation. He and Mary were pledged to be married. But Mary was pregnant, and Joseph knew he wasn't the father! This wasn't an engagement period similar to ours. According to the customs of that time and place, they were considered married with one exception—they would not live together or have a sexual relationship for a period of nine to twelve months to ensure pregnancy was not the reason for marriage. As they were considered married, the relationship could only be broken by divorce. Joseph could sign the legal divorce papers in a private, quiet manner, or he could have Mary judged publicly and she could be stoned to death for adultery. What an incredible situation and decision for this man!

Imagine Joseph pacing the dirt floor, praying for an answer, wanting to make the right decision, and hoping God would clearly disclose the perfect solution, His perfect resolution to the problem. Joseph finally comes to the conclusion that he will divorce Mary quietly and spare her life and her family's humiliation and grief rather than elect the public stoning and humiliation for her family. Finally, exhausted and confused, he slept.

While Joseph was sleeping, God made clear His perfect will. An angel of the Lord appeared to Joseph in a dream and said, "Joseph, son of David, do not fear to take Mary as your wife, for that which is conceived in her is from the Holy Spirit. She will bear a son, and you shall call His name Jesus, for He will save His people from their sins" (Mt 1:20b–21).

What a shock the message and messenger must have been for this man. However, Scripture shows that Joseph was a man of great faith. It simply states that "When Joseph woke from sleep, he did as the angel of the Lord commanded him: he took his wife" (Mt 1:24). He did not question the angel's message. He woke up and did what the angel commanded. A man of great faith, indeed.

Rather than doubt, become bewildered, or even boast, Joseph trusted the angel. His angle on angels was to realize that they are the messengers of God. In obeying the angel, he was obeying the Lord. And what an incredible message the Lord's messenger had for him—the child within Mary was conceived by the Holy Spirit. The child he would father was the heavenly Father's gift of the world's Savior! Yet, seemingly, Joseph had no qualms or questions. The Lord's angelic messenger gave a clear message about what Joseph was to do, and it is clear that Joseph obeyed.

Joseph Had a Strong Faith

God created a strong faith within Joseph. He knew how God had used angels as messengers throughout the history of His people. Joseph's angle on angels was shaped by the truth of God's Word and that God had the power to use any means to share the message of salvation with His people.

Our angle on angels is not one of dreamy little collectibles. Angels are messengers of God who can communicate even to ordinary people like you and me. Yet the importance of the story isn't the angel or Joseph. It is the truth of the angel's message. The angel's message clearly pointed to the One conceived within Mary—the one Joseph must name Jesus.

Just as the word *angel*, which means "messenger," is significant for our angle on angels, the name *Jesus* also tells a story. His name means "Savior." Jesus was born to save His people from their sins. What a story to behold! What a story to be told! Not just the story of Joseph and his angel visitor, but the life-saving, sin-forgiving story of the one named Jesus. His story was foretold by an angel, and it changed history— your history and mine, your future and mine. That's a life-changing angle in which we put our faith.

Advent 2

Mary's Angle

Luke 1:26–38

The e-mail from a friend states: "I need to talk to you tonight. Call me." Or a message may come into your voice mail: "The boss wants to see you immediately." Or a child, spouse, or parent approaches you and says, "We need to talk." These messages sound urgent and ominous. It's easy to imagine the worst and allow anxiety to prevail. Even some persons' mere presence can be troublesome.

But none of those scenarios compares to the story of a teenage girl who meets an intimidating messenger with an intimidating message. Unexpectedly, an angel stands before Mary. We can only imagine how frightened Mary must have been to see this heavenly visitor. But the angel brings a gift to the shaken (and maybe even shaking) teenager, a gift bound in grace. "Do not be afraid, Mary, for you have found favor with God" (Lk 1:30). The gift is peace. If there is anything Mary needs as she listens to the news the angel has for her, it is peace. Mary will need that gift as she heads into the future, carrying and caring for the Prince of Peace. The gift of peace came from the presence of the Lord and His angels.

DO NOT BE AFRAID

"Do not be afraid," the angel told Mary. Through those words, the gift of peace was unwrapped. Mary was transformed from "shaken" to "at peace." The angelic messenger announced that Mary would be the mother of the world's Savior, the mother of a child who also is God. That life-changing news was accompanied with the peace only God could provide. The Lord of compassion used the angel Gabriel to announce that peace. Mary's response to Gabriel showed that transformation from panic to peace. She says, with peaceful confidence, "I am the servant of the Lord; let it be to me according to Your word" (Lk 1:38).

That is a miraculous statement. It can be spoken by Mary because of the miracle of her Spirit-created faith, lined with God's miracle of peace. Mary's angle on angels is that they are God's messengers of peace. Scripture often paints that portrait of angels. When God sends His angels with a message, they often greet the receiver of that message with "Do not be afraid." Angels are to be welcomed, not feared, as messengers of God and His peace.

When Mary realized what lay ahead, she easily could have panicked and succumbed to fear. During the engagement period, she would have to face the embarrassment of her pregnancy, the scorn of unbelieving neighbors, and the responsibility of raising the promised Messiah. Unknown to her at the time, she eventually would also witness her Son's horrible execution.

"Do not be afraid," the angel said. During her lifetime Mary surely replayed those words in her mind time and time again, reopening God's gift of peace. She had the Lord's favor. He would not abandon her as she stepped into the fearful future. Picture an army of angels surrounding Mary as she traveled to Bethlehem to give birth, or as family members abandoned Jesus, or even as she sat at the foot of the cross, where her Son was crucified for her sins and ours.

Respond without Fear

In faith, picture God's army of angels surrounding us. Like Mary, we are undeserving of the Lord's favor, yet we can be at peace in His grace. The Lord is with us. At our Baptism He stood before us, along with His angels, and spoke to us. He welcomed us into His kingdom, forgave our sins, and held open the door to heaven for us. The Lord also has great plans for us. By the power of the Spirit, we are enabled to respond to the Lord's call, "I am the servant of the Lord; let it be to me according to Your word."

As the angel reminded Mary, nothing is impossible with God. Those peace-filled words changed Mary's life, even as Christ lived within her. As Christ lives within us, we are not afraid. Despite situations that evoke fear and uncertainty, keep the right angle on this truth from the angel: the peace of the one named Jesus is with you!

Advent 3

Heaven's Angle

Luke 2:8–14; Hebrews 1:14

It is of great value in my faith walk to consider heaven's angle on various situations. For instance, if someone has mistreated me, I consider how I have treated God through my sinful actions and how He deals with me. He continues to love me and offers forgiveness for my sins. There is no limit to His faithfulness. Considering heaven's angle helps me respond with a Christlike love. As I seek to console another who is grieving because of the death of a family member or friend, I attempt to regard death from heaven's angle. A viewpoint of life, victory, and eternal joy allows me to share that person's grief and yet rejoice in the eternal life of heaven's newest resident.

What is heaven's angle on angels? The inspired author of Hebrews writes, "Are they not all ministering spirits sent out to serve for the sake of those who are to inherit salvation?" (Heb 1:14). Using few words, this verse gives us great heavenly insights regarding angels. They are spirits; they minister; they are sent. They don't act on their own; rather, they follow God's perfect will. They are servants, following the example of heaven's perfect servant, Jesus Christ. And they serve God's dearly beloved children, who will one day inherit heaven, the home of God's angels, His messengers.

In past weeks, God's Word revealed to us that angels were called to serve and minister to Joseph and Mary. The angels played a great role in the preparation of the birth of the Advent King, as well as the birth of the forerunner of Christ, John the Baptizer. Today we draw even closer to the manger. God didn't use just one angel to share the message of Jesus' birth with the shepherds—the news could not be contained in heaven. Tens of thousands of angels announced the Savior's birth, worshiped God, and ministered to the shepherds.

Proclaim the News

Consider heaven's angle on the angels as the Lord of heaven and earth sent them to the fields near Bethlehem. Let your imagination sense heaven's excitement as the eternal, perfect plan of the world's salvation came to fruition that night. The angels, and all the company of heaven, surely desired to proclaim the wondrous news and worship God, evidenced by the way the angels erupted on the scene, singing their praises and announcing peace to the world. Picture the archangel trying to hold back the joy-swelled angels until just the perfect moment when they were called on to fill Bethlehem's night sky!

Listen, again, to the angelic events of that most holy night. First, an angel of the Lord appears to the shepherds. He was heaven's messenger with a heavenly message. Not surprisingly, he first offers them God's perfect peace. "Fear not," he says. Then the greatest birth announcement ever comes in these words: "I bring you good news of a great joy that will be for all the people. For unto you is born this day in the city of David a Savior, who is Christ the Lord. And this will be a sign for you: you will find a baby wrapped in swaddling cloths and lying in a manger" (Lk 2:10–12).

Glory to God

Following that, heaven could not contain the joy of the angels! A great company of the heavenly host—a multitude of angel armies—appeared in the sky. Please note the emphasis of their words. They praised God. The angels did not just dance with glee or sing unintentionally—they praised God. The first words gave glory to whom glory must be given—God their Creator. God, the one they served; God, the one who loved the world so much He sent His only Son to the world to save a multitude of undeserving, sinful people. All the earth must give God glory, for He has favored His people, allowing His perfect peace to rest on them. It is the same favorable peace that rests on us today. With the same joy, it is our pleasure and privilege to give all glory to God. Angels definitely have the right angle on the Advent season—glory goes to God.

To give God glory is to take the servant role and give credit where it is due. Part of our role as Advent messengers is to prepare the world for Christ's return. (This is another wonderful event to imagine from heaven's angle!) In our proclamation of Jesus, are we filled with the same kind of joy as were the Advent angels? Do we worship God with the same joyful, serving heart as the angels? We need to realize we have fallen short in that calling. But when we consider that Jesus was born for those who fall short of His glory and that He offers forgiveness of all our sins, our response grows with joy and glory-filled praise!

Advent is a time of preparing for Christ's coming at Christmas, on the Last Day, and as He comes to us daily through His Word and Sacraments. Through the angels, through His Word and Sacraments, He brings us a message of peace. God's angels surround us. They kneel with us in awe and praise the Lord as we eat and drink the bread and wine, His true body and blood. They stand guard over our minds and hearts as we study His Word, and they stand in awe of His love for us. They set up camp around our life as a baptized child of God. In all situations, consider heaven's right angle on angels—that God sends His ministering angels to serve us constantly. With our lives and voices, we join the angels proclaiming, "Glory to God in the highest, and on earth peace among those with whom He is pleased!" (Lk 2:14).

Hymn Sing Sermons

Rev. D. Lee Cullen Jr.

Advent 1

Christ Our Hope

1 Timothy 1:1

During this season of Advent, by the power of the Spirit, we shall focus on three key words associated with the coming of Christ into our world. Each of these words highlights a particular aspect of the season as well as the blessings that the Christian has through faith in the Savior; namely, hope, joy, and peace. This night our focus is "Christ Jesus our Hope" (1 Tim 1:1).

HOPE IN THE OLD TESTAMENT

The Old Testament is replete with promises and prophecies that point to Christ as the hope of people.

In Genesis there is the sad and tragic story of humankind's fall into sin. Satan had tempted our first parents with false hopes and expectations of greater knowledge, in fact, godlike knowledge. In their weakness, they disobeyed our Lord's command and the pall of hopelessness fell upon the human race. Adam and Eve tried in vain to hide from the Lord, hoping against hope that God would not find out what they had done.

Our gracious Creator did know, and He sought after them. When He found them, God spoke the first promise of the Savior that would fuel the hopes of His people for many years. Through the woman's Seed, the expectation of deliverance from death, salvation from sin, and rescue from the devil became the hope of the people. In fact, so great was Eve's hope for the Savior that when she gave birth to her firstborn son she said, "I have gotten a man with the help of the LORD" (Gen 4:1) or, as Martin Luther translated that verse, "I have the man, the Lord!"

However, many centuries passed before the advent of the promised Seed of the woman. Some four thousand years ago the Almighty gave a promise to a man named Abram, later called Abraham. He promised Abraham he would be the father of countless peoples. However, Abraham had no children, and he and his wife were quite old, past the normal age for bearing children.

The apostle Paul writes, "In hope he believed against hope, that he should become the father of many nations, as he had been told. . . . No distrust made him waver concerning the promise of God" (Rom 4:18, 20). This promise of many children and that one Child in whom the world would be blessed served as the beacon of hope for God's people through the centuries. That Holy Child would be the Savior of the world.

Christ Is Our Savior Too

That promised Seed of the woman, that child of Abraham in whom the world would be blessed, is our Savior too. You and I are a part of the fulfillment of God's promise to Abraham as well as partakers, sharers in the promise of that Descendant, that long-foretold Deliverer born all those years ago.

We are blessed beyond imagination: blessed with pardon from sin, victory over Satan, and hope of eternal life. No wonder we raise our voices with the saints of all ages to our God and Savior, for He kept His promises to send Jesus, the sinner's help and friend.

Sing "Let the Earth Now Praise the Lord" (LSB 352:1, 3, 5).

Having such a wonderful hope set before them, however, did not keep God's chosen people from sinning or straying into the sins of their unbelieving neighbors. Even after they promised to love and to serve God at Mount Sinai and made His covenant of grace with them, they turned and went their own way. The hope of the people was set aside as they placed their hopes in false gods and idols.

Hope in the Midst of Affliction

As you know, God's people endured much chastening by His hand as they were oppressed and conquered and even driven from the Promised Land. Not only were their hopes beginning to dim as they waited for the promised Deliverer to make His appearance, but they also underwent much spiritual affliction. During the lowest moments, Jeremiah reminded Judah that her hope, even in the direst of situations, was still the Lord.

We are no strangers to affliction. Many times our thoughts and feelings mirror those of Jeremiah and the faithful of all the ages who have endured great sorrow and suffering in their lives. And why? Because we live in a sin-fallen world. We may wonder, Will I ever get any relief? Can I really have the hope that things will improve? We, too, may feel somewhat exiled from God and isolated at such times, all the while looking for that light at the end of the tunnel.

We may be wrestling with spiritual weaknesses or struggling with some physical or emotional affliction. Whatever it may be in your life, your hope is in the Lord, who has rescued you from your body of death, promised grace and strength in your hour of trial and affliction, and assured you that all these things will end when He comes again. We long for God to come and work mightily in our lives by His grace.

Sing "O Come, O Come, Emmanuel" (LSB 357:1, 3–4).

Throughout the years preceding the birth of Christ, God revealed through His prophets more specifics regarding the Savior so that the hopes of His people would be kindled and burn brightly. He promised through Isaiah, "The virgin shall conceive and bear a son, and shall call His name Immanuel" (Is 7:14). Through the prophet Micah the Lord pinpointed the place of the Messiah's birth: "But you, O Bethlehem Ephrathah, who are too little to be among the clans of Judah, from you shall come forth for Me one who is to be ruler in Israel, whose origin is from of old, from ancient days" (Micah 5:2).

By the Power of the Spirit

Some seven hundred years later God sent the angel Gabriel to a virgin named Mary, announcing that she would conceive the Savior by the power of the Holy Spirit and bring forth the Promised One into the world. After visiting Elizabeth, Mary sang, "My soul magnifies the Lord, and my spirit rejoices in God my Savior. . . . He has helped His servant Israel, in remembrance of His mercy, as He spoke to our fathers, to Abraham and to His offspring forever" (Lk 1:46–47, 54–55). Nine months later the man Eve had sought, the descendant Abraham looked for, the desire of the nations was born in a little town called Bethlehem, fulfilling the hopes and dreams of God's people.

Sing "O Little Town of Bethlehem" (LSB 361:1, 4).

So what hopes were wrapped up in those swaddling cloths and laid in a manger? The primary hope is crushing Satan's power and rule over the hearts of people by the power of sin.

Enslaved in the Darkness of Sin

From the devil's first deception that led to sin, we were made his captives and were enslaved to darkness, chaffing under the cruel rod of oppression and tyranny. Nothing man could do could deliver himself from the hopeless situation of sin. Man by nature was constrained to do evil and wickedness and had no power to do anything else.

With the advent of Christ, the hopes of one who could contend with the devil and break his power, as well as the power of sin and death, were realized. In this Child born of Mary, the devil was overmatched because Jesus was true God in the flesh, the almighty Lord of hosts. Yet it was not with a flick of His omnipotent hand that He vanquished the devil and broke the power of sin and death. Rather, it was with His hands and feet nailed to a cross that He crushed the serpent's head. By His death and resurrection He broke Satan's back and delivered us from his kingdom of darkness. No longer are you and I captives to the darkness of sin, living in dread of death. For through faith in Christ, the apostle Peter says, "He has caused us to be born again to a living hope through the resurrection of Jesus Christ from the dead" (1 Pet 1:3).

THE HOPE OF ETERNAL LIFE

Because of Jesus, who is the resurrection and the life, you and I have the certain expectation and unwavering hope that we will live though we die, that sin will not get the best of us, and that we will see and be with all who have died in the Lord. We have the certain hope that we will be reunited with our loved ones who have died with Christ and with Christ Himself when He comes again.

Since He is risen and ascended on high, we have the sure promise we will soon join Him. The writer to the Hebrews says, "We have this as a sure and steadfast anchor of the soul" (Heb 6:19). An anchor keeps a vessel firmly moored and fastened so that no matter how fierce the winds may blow and the waves crash against its sides, it will not be moved.

Since we have a living hope in Jesus Christ, our souls are anchored, moored, and fastened to Him who is now even in heaven. Although all the devils and demons rage against us, though we are afflicted with every imaginable disease and suffering, though we are assaulted by doubts and uncertainties, we have Christ as the anchor for our souls always. From Him nothing can move us, not even death itself, because He is our fortress, our trust and hope secure.

Sing "Christ Is the World's Redeemer" (LSB 539:1, 3–4).

Since Christ is our hope, giving to us the confident and sure expectation of everlasting life with Him, we may cling to this hope and hold onto it for dear life as though nothing else matters in the entire world. For without hope of deliverance from this world's woes, without hope of the resurrection and restoration of our bodies, without hope of a wonderful reunion with the saints in heaven, without hope of eternal salvation, and without Christ in our lives, our lives would certainly be miserable, aimless, and meaningless.

LIVING WITHOUT HOPE

Have you ever seen anyone living without hope? Their faces and countenances are usually drawn, their lives listless since they have no anchor for their souls. They go through life dreading life and death. Although there are times when our hope in Christ is fiercely challenged, we know that in Christ our lives have meaning and purpose because "by the power of the Holy Spirit [we] may abound in hope" (Rom 15:13).

SHARE THE MESSAGE OF HOPE

St. Peter says that we are always to be ready to give an answer to everyone who asks for a reason for the hope that is in us. In other words, we are always to be prepared to speak to others about Christ our hope, and why we are confident and certain that God is with us in good and bad times and will take us to be with Him on the Last Day.

We are to tell them how Jesus is the answer to the hopes of not only those Old Testament people of God but also of you and me, His New Testament people, who now await His second advent. We are to tell them they can share in the same hope through faith in Jesus by the power of the Spirit.

THE FINAL ADVENT OF CHRIST

As the Old Testament people waited in fervent expectation for the Savior's birth, we now look in eager anticipation for His return. When our long-expected Jesus comes again, we will be free from sin forever. Then we will no longer be tempted and accused by the devil. Then we will live in glory with all who, like us, had lived in hope.

Sing "Come, Thou Long-Expected Jesus" (LSB 22:1–2).

Advent 2

Christ Our Joy

Luke 2:10–11

Last week we focused on "Christ Our Hope" as we await His second and final advent into our world. Tonight we turn our attention to that glad news foretold through the centuries by the prophets, announced by the angels and shepherds at the first Christmas, and still proclaimed by the Christian Church today.

Luke writes: "The angel said to them, 'Fear not, for behold, I bring you good news of a great joy that will be for all the people. For unto you is born this day in the city of David a Savior, who is Christ the Lord.' " (Lk 2:10–11). In word and in song this night we celebrate the Good News of "Christ Our Joy."

Our Joy in Jesus

As we look around the world today and at our own lives, we may wonder if there is cause for joy. Perhaps not, for the world's idea of joy is radically different from the true joy the believer already possesses by faith in Christ. The joy that the Bible speaks about, which is ours in Jesus, transcends even the loftiest of the world's ideals, just as Christian hope does.

The world's idea of joy is to have one's fancy tickled, to be amused, to be made happy and merry whatever it takes. As long as people get their way, as long as things are rosy, then the world thinks there is cause for joy. In fact, from the opening chapters to the end of the Bible we find the opposite is true. When man gets his way, when one's sinful self directs life and actions to pursue joy and self-satisfaction, misery and sorrow often follow. Sin and living in a sinful world interferes and hinders the joy God gives us to experience in our lives.

Now, because of the consequences of sin, mothers have great pain before the birth of a child and the joy that accompanies that event. Now, because creation groans under the corruption brought on by sin, man must labor and toil before partaking of the earth's bounty. Yet even more oppression lies in wait for man because of the weight of sin. Sin, whether it be our own or another's, brings misery, suffering, sorrow, and death into all of our lives without exception.

These circumstances do much to mute and hinder our joy and the living out of that joy in our lives. However, God has never left His creation desolate and despairing. Rather, to Adam and Eve, to Abraham and his descendants, and throughout the Old Testament God promised to send a Savior, one who would deliver them from the misery and captivity of their sin, one who would bind up their wounds and give them gladness in the place of sadness.

The Prophets Speak of Joy

Isaiah speaks of this Savior when he writes these words of our Lord speaking of Himself and His work:

> The Spirit of the Lord GOD is upon Me, because the LORD has anointed Me to bring good news to the poor; He has sent Me to bind up the brokenhearted, to proclaim liberty to the captives, and the opening of the prison to those who are bound; to proclaim the year of the LORD's favor, and the day of vengeance of our God; to comfort all who mourn; to grant to those who mourn in Zion—to give them a beautiful headdress instead of ashes, the oil of gladness instead of mourning, the garment of praise instead of a faint spirit. (Is 61:1–3)

Similarly, the prophet Zechariah called on the people in their struggles and trials as they sought to rebuild the temple after their exile to rejoice in the coming of this King. Even in their affliction and sorrow, Zechariah urged them to reclaim the joy that was theirs in the Messiah: "Rejoice greatly, O daughter of Zion! Shout aloud, O daughter of Jerusalem! behold, your king is coming to you; righteous and having salvation is He" (Zech 9:9). In the promised Savior true joy is found and given because He is the one who takes away our mourning, our misery, our sadness and replaces it with rest, joy, and gladness. Great was their anticipation and joy for that day when their King would come, mighty to save.

Sing "O Come, O Come, Emmanuel" (LSB 357:1, 5–6).

As you well know, Israel had some very dark days in her history. When she sinned against the Lord she was oppressed by the Canaanite peoples, split into two kingdoms, ruled by wicked, unscrupulous kings, and eventually conquered and exiled from her land. Anguish and lament were certainly the rule of the day as she endured chastisements and tribulations.

REJOICE IN THE FACE OF SUFFERING

We also have dark days, days when Murphy's Law seems in effect more than usual, when joy seems far from our lives. Whether we struggle with physical ailments, with depression or other mental ailments, or with the sorrows we see family and friends experiencing, joy and gladness often seem difficult to find, let alone show forth.

Our Lord is not oblivious to this. He knows that living in a sin-filled world, coping with bodies and minds corrupted by sin, and enduring the trials of life can make it appear that joy is far from our lives. He knows because He Himself also lived in this world and experienced its sorrows and grief as our Savior. Isaiah reminds us: "He was . . . a man of sorrows, and acquainted with grief. . . . Surely He has borne our griefs and carried our sorrows. . . . He was oppressed, and He was afflicted" (Is 53:3–4, 7).

Because our Lord has already endured great suffering and sorrow Himself on our behalf, because we are not alone in our sorrow and sadness, the writers of Holy Scripture urge you and me to rejoice and to be glad in our lives. That is not always easy when we are in the shadows of our life or wrestling with the woes of life.

Yet it is precisely in these circumstances that we are urged to rejoice and to be joyful, for we know that the Lord is with us, that He sympathizes with us and reaches out to us with love. St. James writes, "Count it all joy, my brothers, when you meet trials of various kinds" (1:2). The apostle Paul echoes that sentiment when he writes, "Rejoice in the Lord always; again I will say, Rejoice" (Phil 4:4) and "Rejoice always" (1 Thess 5:16). Such language is incomprehensible to a world that equates joy with outward circumstances, appearances, and places in life.

Joy Is Grounded in the Lord

For the believer, though, joy is not evaluated by such shifting standards of human whim and fickleness. Rather, joy for the Christian is grounded in his Lord, who remains for him a refuge and an ever-present help in time of need. Joy for the disciple is realized in his Lord, who gives him rest from his burdens as God lifts us up as on wings of an eagle. Joy for the redeemed is assured because our Savior God has promised to keep us by His power through faith for salvation.

None of life's woes, sorrows, or afflictions can take away the joy that we have in Christ nor prevent us from inheriting the joy that awaits us in His eternal kingdom. This, St. Peter says, is cause for rejoicing, even if we are grieved for a little while by trials now, because then, on the Great Day of our Lord, our joy will be made full and last for all eternity.

The Savior promised and born long ago assures us of salvation and delivers us from evil. This is the news of comfort and joy the believer needs to hear and be reminded of in his life so that he does not become dismayed. These are the glad tidings of comfort and joy that remain ours even today, giving us rest and making us merry during the storms while we await the everlasting rest and joys of heaven.

Sing "God Rest You Merry, Gentlemen" (traditional).

As the people filed to their hometowns to pay their taxes as Caesar had decreed, I suspect their lives were far from joyful. Imagine, though, the buzz and the excitement in Bethlehem as all those people milled about their ancestral town—all that hustle and bustle and stress and exasperation.

How different the scene must have been in the countryside when our Savior was born. In some cave used as a shelter by shepherds, the Lord of glory lay in a crude bed. There He was, the one who gave and still gives joy to all who experience the second birth in His name. In Him is found the reconciliation of the world, the full and free salvation of men. He is the one who gives light and life, freeing us from the darkness of sin and death.

What joy erupts in our hearts when we ponder the birth of our Savior and peer in His cradle. What joy is ours today and for all our life to know that in Jesus all our guilt and shame are removed. In this Holy Babe, God gives the joy of salvation to each believing sinner. Like the prisoner who is released from his cell and given a new lease on life is so happy he can hardly contain himself, so also are we released from sin's power and given new life by this Babe born of Mary. He gives us a joy only possible in Christ.

With Joy Adore the Living Lord

In the incarnate Son of God, who lay before us in Bethlehem's manger, judgment for our sin is cast out, our reconciliation with God is effected, and our enemies are routed and overthrown. In Jesus Christ, God gives us joy and hearts for rejoicing as Zephaniah the prophet writes: "Sing aloud, O daughter of Zion; shout, O Israel! Rejoice and exult with all your heart, O daughter of Jerusalem! The LORD has taken away the judgments against you; He has cleared away your enemies. The King of Israel, the LORD, is in your midst" (Zeph 3:14–15).

What greater cause for joy can we have? What greater reason to rejoice can we find? What greater justification to shout out and be glad can be offered? Christ is in our midst. He lives in our hearts by His Spirit. He has taken away the judgment against our sin. He has defeated and broken the devil and the grave by His death and resurrection from the dead. He has made us to share in His victory, His joy, His life. He has made us citizens of heaven. Oh, come, all ye faithful, joyful and triumphant! Oh, come, let us adore Him!

Sing "O Come, All Ye Faithful" (LSB 379:1–3).

And in the same region there were shepherds out in the field, keeping watch over their flock by night. And an angel of the Lord appeared to them, and the glory of the Lord shone around them, and they were filled with fear. And the angel said to them, "Fear not, for behold, I bring you good news of a great joy that will be for all the people. For unto you is born this day in the city of David a Savior, who is Christ the Lord." . . . And when they saw [Jesus], they made known the saying that had been told them concerning this child. (Lk 2:8–11, 17)

SHARING THE JOY

The joy those shepherds experienced on seeing the Savior the first Christmas was so great they could not keep it to themselves. Like a child who gets a star on his paper, the shepherds went out and told everyone they met about the Child born of Mary, who was born to be the Savior of the world.

Indeed, the Church today is still in the business of spreading that same joy. As those who have heard and believed the news about the Child of Mary, we are to repeat the joy and repeat it and repeat it and repeat it. We are to proclaim and to shout from the mountaintops how that Child, the Son of God born of the Virgin Mary, was born into the world to deliver all humanity from the misery of sin and to give them the joys of His kingdom.

We are to tell others how this Jesus, "who for the joy that was set before Him endured the cross, despising the shame, and is seated at the right hand of the throne of God" (Heb 12:2), so that they may repent and believe in Him. We are to spread the news of the joy there is in heaven when one sinner repents in order to comfort a brother and sister overtaken by sin. We are to take Christ our Joy to the world so that others may have what we and countless saints through the ages have had—joy in the forgiveness of sins, joy in our coming salvation, joy in the trials and sorrows of life, joy in heaven forever. "Joy to the world, the Lord is come!"

we sing. Let us proclaim Him to the world, as did the shepherds of old, that people may hear and believe in Him born in Bethlehem to be their Savior and ours. *Sing "Joy to the World" (LSB 387:1–2).*

Advent 3

Christ Our Peace

Micah 5:5a; Ephesians 2:14a

From the earliest peace treaties to the ongoing Israeli-Palestinian accords, there have been many human attempts to establish peace in this world. Since the fall of Adam and Eve into sin, there is without doubt a need for peace in this world, in our nation, and even in our own lives, evidenced by the tumult and unrest in the lives of people throughout the pages of Holy Scripture.

Adam and Eve have the first marital discord. They are the first to "pass the buck" and to point fingers at one another. So corrupted was Cain's heart by sin that he murdered his brother, Abel. Jacob was forced to run for his life after deceiving his brother.

SOMETIMES PEACE IS ELUSIVE

Especially during stressful and hectic moments in our lives, a certain unrest and tumult will arise and peace seems nowhere to be found. Especially when we are confronted with our sinful weaknesses and are downcast and feeling low, peace remains elusive in our lives. In truth, we are at war with God in heaven. We fired the first volley, rebelling against His will and turning away from our loving, gracious Creator. As a result, the absence of peace in our world or our own souls finds its source in sin.

GOD INITIATES PEACE

The Lord God Almighty could have destroyed all of humanity; instead, He chose to establish peace with us, providing the means by which this peace with Him would be obtained. He Himself fulfilled the terms for our peace and now gives us the benefits of His peacemaking work by grace through faith in His Son.

THE PRINCE OF PEACE

Our peace was placed in one man, but one who is more than a man. Isaiah writes this about Christ our Peace: "For to us a child is born, to us a son is given; and the government shall be upon His shoulder, and His name shall be called Wonderful Counselor, Mighty God, Everlasting Father, Prince of Peace. Of the increase of His government and of peace there will be no end" (Is 9:6–7).

Micah, a prophet who lived during the same time as Isaiah, writes this about Christ our Peace:

> But you, O Bethlehem Ephrathah, who are too little to be among the clans of Judah, from you shall come forth for Me one who is to be ruler in Israel, whose origin is from of old, from ancient days. Therefore He shall give them up until the time when she who is in labor has given birth; then the rest of His brothers shall return to the people of Israel. And He shall stand and shepherd His flock in the strength of the LORD, in the majesty of the name of the LORD His God. And they shall dwell secure, for now He shall be great to the ends of the earth. And He shall be their peace. (Micah 5:2–5a)

Nearly seven hundred years later, the voice of one crying in the wilderness was born to herald the Prince of Peace's arrival to His people. This is what John the Baptist's father said at John's circumcision:

> And you, child, will be called the prophet of the Most High; for you will go before the Lord to prepare His ways, to give knowledge of salvation to His people in the forgiveness of their sins, because of the tender mercy of our God, whereby the sunrise shall visit us from on high to give light to those who sit in darkness and in the shadow of death, to guide our feet into the way of peace. (Lk 1:76–79)

What a glad sound for the people to hear. The Prince of Peace promised long ago had come into our world.

Sing "Hark the Glad Sound" (LSB 349:1, 4).

THE CHURCH'S CALL
TO PROCLAIM THE PEACE OF CHRIST

Throughout the history of salvation God called on His prophets and people to speak of peace and comfort to His people. This is the message that is necessary for every heart besieged by sin and weighed down by guilt. This is the glad news that the tormented and conflicted soul requires for healing and rest.

All of us desire rest and peace from a variety of sorrows and afflictions of life, release from our sin, a refuge from the woe and grief of life. In Christ, God provides just that. No, He hasn't taken us out of the world. The peace given us in Christ is not as the world gives.

Rather, the peace God gives in Christ Jesus is the comfort that is ours in knowing all our iniquity, all our transgressions, all our sins are pardoned by God in heaven. When we are in Christ, we are no longer at war with God. Through faith in Christ as the ransom for our sins, God has declared peace with us. He has declared an end to the enmity that came about because of our sin. He has established a new relationship with Him for us in Christ Jesus.

This is the message that the Church throughout the ages is to declare to those under the weight of sin, the burden of guilt, and the curse of the Law. This is what our Lord foretold John the Baptist would do as he preceded Christ. This is what our Lord would have us do as Isaiah writes: " 'Comfort, comfort My people,' says your God. Speak tenderly to Jerusalem, and cry to her that her warfare is ended, that her iniquity is pardoned, that she has received from the LORD's hand double for all her sins" (Is 40:1–2).

Sing "Comfort, Comfort Ye My People" (LSB 347:1–2).

THE PRICE OF PEACE

This peace and reconciliation that God established with us in Christ did have its price. Just as bloodshed, loss, and casualties precede the peace that follows war and conflict in our world, so also was our peace with God accomplished. God's peace for the world was accomplished through the blood-soaked cross lifted up on Calvary's hill with His only-begotten Son nailed to it.

Isaiah had foretold this when he wrote: "We esteemed Him stricken, smitten by God, and afflicted. But He was wounded for our transgressions; He was crushed for our iniquities; upon Him was the chastisement that brought us peace" (Is 53:4–5). Paul adds, "For in Him all the fullness of God was pleased to dwell, and through Him to reconcile to Himself all things . . . making peace by the blood of His cross" (Col 1:19–20). Because of this sacrificial life and death of Christ our Peace, our warfare with God is declared obsolete and at an end.

The angels proclaimed that on the night of Jesus' birth. In the Child of Mary peace came to earth and God's goodwill, His desire to effect reconciliation with humanity, was demonstrated. Through faith in Jesus the believer personally has this peace with God as St. Paul writes, "Therefore, since we have been justified by faith, we have peace with God through our Lord Jesus Christ" (Rom 5:1). It is a present reality; that is, every believer, having been justified and pardoned through Jesus Christ, has peace with God right now and the promise of everlasting peace in the heavenly Jerusalem. No wonder we still sing the angels' words giving glory to God for giving us peace on earth and in heaven in Christ our Peace.

Sing "Hark! The Herald Angels Sing" (LSB 380:1–3).

Christ's Peace Is for All

The promises of peace and reconciliation with God are intended for all people. Again, the apostle Paul writes, "Therefore remember that at one time you Gentiles in the flesh . . . who once were far off have been brought near by the blood of Christ. For He Himself is our peace" (Eph 2:11, 13–14). Each one of us is a part of that great Gentile throng who have received peace in the Lord Christ.

That, perhaps, was seen initially through the visit of the Gentiles from the east who bowed down and worshiped at the feet of the Prince of Peace. St. Matthew writes, "After Jesus was born in Bethlehem of Judea in the days of Herod the king, behold, wise men from the east came to Jerusalem, saying, 'Where is He who has been born king of the Jews? For we saw His star when it rose and have come to worship Him' " (Mt 2:1–2).

As the song we will sing recognizes, Christ Jesus came into the world so that all people, Jew and Gentile alike, would have peace with God in heaven. The King of kings and Lord of lords is born into the world to draw all persons, prince and pauper, young and old, men and women, to Himself. As you sing "We Three Kings," do so in the perspective that you are walking in their shoes by God's grace to heaven's perfect light because Christ our Peace came for all people.

Sing "We Three Kings" (traditional).

Peace That Passes All Understanding

St. Paul's words to the Church at Philippi provide assurance and comfort: "The peace of God, which surpasses all understanding, will guard your hearts and your minds in Christ Jesus" (Phil 4:7). God gives us the assurance that through Jesus nothing can keep us from the eternal rest and solace He has laid up for us in heaven with Him.

It is that quiet confidence and surety, beyond our explanation, that comforts our hearts even in the most trying circumstance. It is that unseen strength and hope that causes our spirits to soar and to rejoice in our Redeemer. It is Jesus Himself. It is Christ who is our Hope, our Joy, and our Peace for this life and the next. We celebrate with the angels Christ's salvation and await that day of glory when we shall join them in heaven's choir.

Sing "It Came upon the Midnight Clear" (LSB 366:1, 3–4).

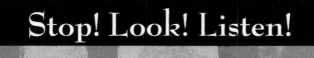

Stop! Look! Listen!

Stop!

Isaiah 1:16b–17a, 18

Is a little fear good at times? According to a newspaper article, in 1850 the United States government established a new commission that regulated lighthouses. This commission was required to make lighthouse inspections—rigorous, "white glove" inspections! The lighthouse keepers lived in fear of the time that these inspectors would come by ship. They would inspect the lighthouse facility, evaluate the lighthouse keepers, and even check out the lighthouse keepers' families. These inspections were so feared that keepers of one lighthouse longed to get word to neighboring lighthouses so that people might be prepared for the coming of the inspector. Of course, unless one lighthouse was in sight of another, this was virtually impossible in days before the telephone. As a result, the lighthouse keepers kept everything neat and clean, and even more important, functioning perfectly even in the worst weather.

Years later, one of the descendants of the keeper of a lighthouse said, "It was sort of like the coming of God. It was like the second return of Christ." The article concluded by suggesting that perhaps a little fear is good at times.

FEAR THE LORD'S JUDGMENT

Some of the harshest words spoken by God are recorded in Scripture through the Old Testament prophets. They are intended to instill, among other things, fear in the hearts and the minds of wayward people. On many occasions, God breathed out warnings of impending punishment and judgment on people who had turned from Him toward other gods and had done all of the things that God said that they were never to do. God was not just going to sit idly by and let this happen. Instead He warned, threatened, and even promised punishment for the purpose of instilling fear that the people might repent and seek God once again.

In the first chapter of his book, the prophet Isaiah spoke the Word of the Lord to the people, "Remove the evil of your deeds from before My eyes; cease to do evil, learn to do good" (vv. 16b–17a). These words of God are important for us to hear as surely as they were for ancient Israel.

DISTRACTED BY WORLDLY VALUES

Is a little fear good at times? It is easy to become preoccupied with worldly values and priorities that detract us from what is good and right and pleasing to God. Satan seems to work overtime to distract us especially from those festivals that focus on the core of our faith.

Should not God be disgusted with His people whose focus and energy are on pursuing that which really has no lasting value and no great significance as far as our relationship with Him is concerned? Should not God be upset with us and speak hard words of judgment when we don't recognize the value and importance of maintaining a meaningful relationship with Him? He has entrusted to us countless resources. He has given to us His Word. He reminds us that we are His baptized people, and He offers us regularly the forgiveness of sins through the Holy Supper. Yet so often, we are interested in everything else but that which God uses to draw us close to Him. Should not God become upset with us, saying to us, "Remove the evil of your deeds from before My eyes; cease to do evil, learn to do good"?

The problem is that we suffer from a certain kind of heart trouble, which we cannot fix by ourselves.

Frederick Buechner, when asked how his father died, would answer, "He died of heart trouble." His father had come from a prominent family. His parents had high expectations for him. In school, he was a very good student. At the university, he excelled above most of his classmates, and everybody expected him to have a brilliant career in business. He married and had a family. But when the Great Depression came, it hit him especially hard. He was depressed because he could not achieve the success he felt was expected. Early one morning, he went to the garage and quietly closed the door. He started up his old Chevrolet, sat down on the running board, and put his head in his hands.

His family found him asphyxiated. When asked how his father died, Frederick Buechner would respond, "He died of heart trouble."

THE MESSAGE OF JUDGMENT IS MATCHED BY GOD'S MERCY

The message through Isaiah is not only that we "cease to do evil, learn to do good," but we also hear the Lord speak this through the words of Isaiah, "Come now, let us reason together, says the LORD: though your sins are like scarlet, they shall be as white as snow; though they are red like crimson, they shall become like wool" (v. 18).

By our sinful natures, we no more can live in the way that pleases Him than the sun can stop shining or the world can stop turning. If there is any hope of salvation, it has to come from Him. The good news always is that God is filled with love and compassion and pity and mercy for His people. God could have simply said, "I have had it with the people of Israel," turned away, and let things take their natural course. The people would quickly have come to their destruction and utter oblivion. Rather, God came to them with a message of hope and the promise of a Savior. Today, we have the privilege of looking back two thousand years to the time when God kept His promise, the time when His Son came, the time when God fulfilled through His Son every single requirement necessary for the salvation of every single human being.

Stop!

There is a special need for us as God's people living today to stop what we are doing so that we may, by the power of the Holy Spirit, recognize once again what is right and proper and good for ourselves each day we live. We are God's enlightened people. By God's grace we have come to know the true God and His Son, Jesus Christ. And yet at times we are inclined to head a different direction than is pleasing to God. How important it is for us to stop: to listen to what God is saying to us; to remember that we are children of God; to understand what God expects of us, His people who are living in this sinful, troubled world.

We Are the Light of the World

In His Sermon on the Mount (Mt 5–7) Jesus calls His followers "the salt of the earth" (Mt 5:13) and "the light of the world" (Mt 5:14). He has given us great responsibilities and, at the same time, has high expectations, for He has given us His Spirit. He provides us with the power and the strength needed to make a powerful impact on the world in which we live, so that other people may come to know the compassion and the mercy of almighty God.

This time of Advent, "Stop, Look, and Listen," and prepare for the coming of the Lord.

Advent 2

Look!

John 1:29

We use binoculars, microscopes, telescopes, and magnifying glasses to assist us in seeing certain objects: binoculars for those times when we are hunting or when we are sitting in the "nosebleed section" at an athletic event; microscopes to examine objects that are very small or that the unaided human eye cannot see; telescopes to see stars and other planets in the universe that God has created; magnifying glasses to help us work with something small or read print that is too tiny for our vision. When we see through any of these instruments, we may say to someone, "Look! It's right there. Can't you see it?"

ADVENT IS A TIME FOR REPENTANCE

"Stop, Look, and Listen!" is the overall theme for our worship during this season of Advent. Last week, the focus was on the Word of the Lord, who spoke through the prophet Isaiah, "Remove the evil of your deeds from before My eyes; cease to do evil, learn to do good" (Is 1:16b–17a). Advent is, indeed, a season of repentance, a time when God desires that we examine our thoughts, words, and deeds.

As we look at ourselves with the mirror of the Law, the Ten Commandments, we see very clearly that we have sinned and disobeyed God in many ways. The Law reminds us that we are selfish, self-centered, sinful people who spend much of our time looking out only for our own interests and welfare. The Holy Spirit uses the Law to expose any notions we might have that we're not all that bad.

When we become aware of our sinfulness, we sometimes look in one of three wrong directions.

First, when confronted by our sin and how offensive it is to God, we look only at our sins and dwell on them. When this happens, it is easy to feel hopeless and overwhelmed by our sin and by what we deserve from God. It is easy to think that we are beyond His forgiveness.

Second, when confronted with our sinfulness, we are tempted to look for hope in places not God-directed. For instance, some people will look for hope to the Law, which has convicted them of sin. They reason if they try harder, they can do enough so that God will overlook their sins.

Third, sometimes we blind ourselves with denial and hardened hearts that reject God's Law and Word as they confront our sinfulness. We may look to ourselves for truth and wisdom in order to avoid criticism from others or other potentially painful consequences. We may distort what we've done or not done. We may lie to get others to see us as something that we are not.

Look to Jesus!

When we face the reality of our sinfulness, God does not want us to dwell on and look only at our sins. He does not want us to look for hope in the Law or from false gods. There is no hope for salvation or joy in the Law. The Law makes us aware of our sins. And God does not want us to deny our sinfulness. Instead, God calls us to look to Jesus Christ alone for forgiveness and salvation. When John the Baptist saw Jesus coming toward him, he exclaimed, "Behold, the Lamb of God, who takes away the sin of the world!" (Jn 1:29).

John spoke these words the day after the priests and Levites asked him if he was the Christ—that is, the one chosen by God to be the Savior. John did not look at this as an opportunity to bring glory to himself, but rather told them, "I am not the Christ" (1:20). Like so many others, John had been waiting for the coming of the One who had been promised by God—the sacrificial Lamb—the One the prophet Isaiah wrote about who would come into this world and would be oppressed and afflicted and slaughtered, taking on Himself the punishment we deserve.

John himself had been looking for the coming of the Savior. When John baptized Jesus in the Jordan River, he was certain that Jesus was the one chosen by God to be the Savior of the world. He said, "I saw the Spirit descend from heaven like a dove, and it remained on Him. I myself did not know Him, but He who sent me to baptize with water said to me, 'He on whom you see the Spirit descend and remain, this is He who baptizes with the Holy Spirit.' " When he saw the dove and heard the voice from heaven, John knew he was right. He said, "I have seen and have borne witness that this is the Son of God" (Jn 1:32–34).

In Faith, We See Jesus

As the Son of God, true God and true man, Jesus has accomplished for us what we in our sinfulness can never do. As the Lamb of God He has made possible the cleansing forgiveness that we need. By His perfect obedience of the Law and His death, Jesus has made that forgiveness possible. By His blood He purifies us from all sin.

God the Holy Spirit opens our eyes to all that Jesus has done for us and brings us out of the spiritual darkness and deadness in which we were born and into the light and life of salvation. Through the water of our Baptism the Spirit brings us to faith in Jesus Christ and enables us to look only to Christ as the Lamb of God who not only takes away the sins of the world but also takes away your sins and my sins and the punishment that we deserve from God for them. He opens our hearts and our eyes to the truth of what He says in His Word—certainly about our sinfulness and how He would have us live, but also the truth that we need look no farther than Jesus for forgiveness, eternal life, and salvation.

"Behold, the Lamb of God, who takes away the sin of the world!" The writer of the Epistle to the Hebrews says, "Looking to Jesus, the founder and perfecter of our faith, who for the joy that was set before Him endured the cross, despising the shame, and is seated at the right hand of the throne of God" (12:2). Indeed, let us look to Jesus. Thanks be to God that because of Jesus, we may look forward to eternal life in heaven.

Advent 3

Listen!

Mark 9:7b

There's a three-letter word that describes the month of December more accurately than any other word. In fact, this little word could be the essence of modern American life in this twenty-first century. Here it is *(hold up a card with "DIN" printed on it)*. The word is *din*. Do you know it?

THE DIN IN OUR LIVES

A *din* is a loud, continuing, overwhelming noise. In many households, the radio or television is turned on first thing in the morning. At times, getting the children ready for school or ourselves ready for work can be a continuum of reminders and noises. The sounds of the water in the shower or splashing in the sink, rattling dishes and silverware, soon give way to the roar of children on the school bus. Din! There's Muzak in the factory, in the grocery store, at the mall, and in the office. You can't even escape it in the elevator! Sometimes we can even hear the mind-numbing thumping of music from the car next to us at a stop light—with the windows rolled up! Even joggers and walkers have their music plugged into their ears as they exercise—so much for a quiet walk in the park. Din, my friends, din! Self-imposed din! It's as if we were afraid of any silence at all, as if we would be hopelessly unplugged if we weren't tuned in to our music, our friends, or the latest news story.

Yes, our lives can be a din. And, often, December brings the worst din of all! Add to the normal routines all of the holiday preparations, shopping, and music, and you have a recipe for a kind of cacophony that can drive you to distraction! That is the problem—distraction.

LISTEN TO THE VOICE OF GOD

In the Old Testament Elijah was told, " 'Go out and stand on the mount before the LORD.' And behold, the LORD passed by, and a great and strong wind tore the mountains and broke in pieces the rocks before the LORD, but the LORD was not in the wind. And after the wind an earthquake, but the LORD was not in the earthquake. And after the earthquake a fire, but the LORD was not in the fire. And after the fire the sound of a low whisper" (1 Ki 19:11–12). And that was the voice of God.

Could there be a better appearance of the Lord God in human form than we await this Advent season? God came as a child—the still, small voice of a child.

It is no coincidence that centuries later, on another mountain, Elijah appeared with Moses and with Jesus to hear once again the Word and command of almighty God: "This is My beloved Son; listen to Him" (Mk 9:7b).

We are in great danger if we allow the din of December to drive us to distraction. We might miss the voice. We might miss the message. That is why this Advent season we are called to "Stop, Look, and Listen." Look closely at the pins and decorations we are wearing now. Several of you probably are wearing a pin that says "Jesus is the reason for the season." It's a good reminder, and a necessary one. What does it mean?

JESUS IS THE WORD MADE FLESH

Almost fifty years ago, a man named Marshall McLuhan wrote the book *Understanding Media* in which he coined the phrase "the medium is the message." McLuhan's work helped define an age in our history in which messages were no longer imprisoned in prose neatly typeset in ordered paragraphs and chapters. Today, messages have become piggybacked to electrons in wires and images on television screens, in subliminal messages and advertisements, in graphics and computers, e-mails and spam, Web pages and PowerPoint presentations. These media have created a din of their own that once again threatens to drive us to distraction—distraction from God's own message. Truly, God knows what McLuhan tried to say, but God knew it two thousand years earlier. The first chapter of the Gospel of John gives a name to Jesus that makes it unmistakable. This name is "the Word." Jesus is called "the Word." John's Gospel begins, "In the beginning was the Word, and the Word was with God, and the Word was God" (v. 1).

When God gave us the message of His love, He didn't send us a din of confusing noise and conflicting messages. His message came in the still, small voice of a Child. His message came to us in the form of communication itself, a human Child destined not to just tell of God's love, but to be God's love for us. You see, God's medium is God's message. That is why our theme tonight is "Listen!" Don't miss it. Don't miss "the Word."

Give yourself a Christmas present this year. Let it be the message that Christ came to bring. If you want, take your own Bible, wrap it up in beautiful paper, and put it under your Christmas tree. Where the tag says "To," write your name. Where the tag says "From," write "God." You won't be surprised when you unwrap it, but you will be enlightened as you listen to the message of God. You will be reminded that amid the din of this Christmas season, God's gift to you is a message of love in the person of His Son, Jesus. It is as if God stands behind the manger of Bethlehem, extends His hands on either side of the infant Christ, and says, "This is My beloved Son; listen to Him."

Christmas Eve

The Time Came

Luke 2:1–20

One Christmas, some years back, one of my children expressed a feeling we've all shared. She said, "I wish Christmas time would never be over." Christmas seems to come earlier every year (the commercialization of it, that is). It is a time that comes and goes, leaving us yearning for a day when time would stand still and somehow our lives would be filled with excitement, and our days would be more kind, more lovely, more peaceful. That time never seems to come, though we never give up the dream.

What would life be like without special moments? For example, just think about how this time of the year dominates our days. It's Christmas time, winter-time, shopping time, vacation time. Every day there comes a time to wake up, a time to go to work, a time to eat, a time to play, a time to go to bed. The word *time* defines our existence, as the preacher in the book of Ecclesiastes puts it: "For everything there is a season, and a time for every matter under heaven: a time to be born, and a time to die; . . . a time to weep, and a time to laugh; . . . a time to seek, and a time to lose; . . . a time to love, and a time to hate" (3:1, 2, 4, 6, 8). Those are the times that come and go as we move through life—happy times, sad times, exciting times, boring times, full times, empty times.

And so it is in the world in which we live, marking our time every moment of every day. We are creatures bound by time, which can be a challenge or a problem, an opportunity or a disaster. Time, which was intended by our Creator to be a blessing, sometimes seems to be more like a curse. We delight in those moments when we have good times, exhilarating times, hopeful times. But we can easily turn them into anxious, stressful, hurtful, desperate times.

In the Christmas story, the time came. It came as a decree from the emperor requiring everyone to return to his ancestral hometown for a census. Today the Census Bureau sends representatives to our houses. In those days, they required families to take the time to make a long, hard journey. For shepherds it was time to keep watch over the flocks at night, shivering in the cold, enduring the time until morning came. And for the holy couple, Joseph and Mary, it was time to find a place—not just to rest, but to deliver a baby, since there was no room at the inn. What a time that must have been!

But wait. All of that was setting the stage for an in-breaking (pardon the pun), for an event that would change all time, all our times. "While they were there, the time came for her to give birth" (v. 6). And it's an angel that announces the meaning of that time and event. So significant was the birth of Jesus, an angel was sent to declare, "I bring you good news of a great joy that will be for all the people. For unto you is born this day in the city of David a Savior, who is Christ the Lord" (vv. 10–11). Another messenger of God—the apostle Paul—wrote to the Church in Galatia, "But when the fullness of time had come, God sent forth His Son, born of woman, born under the law, to redeem those who were under the law, so that we might receive adoption as sons" (Gal 4:4–5). The Christmas we celebrate is a moment in time so unique, so decisive, that it is not possible for us in the space of an evening's liturgy to capture the full meaning of this event. That is really what our lifetime is for—to know that time, to love that time, to live that time. Whatever times come, that time changes all our times.

There are four times that are the most significant in all of history—all of them God's times. The first is the time of creation. Nobody was there to observe it, to videotape it. The time came when God created, and the best we can do is marvel at God's mighty works. He continues to sustain His creation, moving it toward His intended goal. We are part and parcel of that process. The second time came when Jesus was born. The love of God took the shape of one named Jesus, born of Mary, but called also Immanuel—God with us—thus blessing and redeeming our times. The third time came when Jesus was raised from death, starting a new creation that surpasses even what happened in the beginning, revealing to us the goal of all humanity, your future and mine. Jesus was born to redeem us, to fulfill all time and deliver all things to His Father. The fourth and final time, yet to arrive but already coming, is Christ's return, which the Church calls the Second Advent—an event that will take place at the conclusion of time as we know it. For us who trust in Christ, it will begin a time of peace and joy forevermore. It will be the fulfillment of that which we celebrate in the Eucharist.

For the millions of believers in Christ, tonight is the culmination of much wishing and hoping and waiting. Christmas means that what we yearn for has already come, is here right now: God is present, with us, with an everlasting love in each and every moment of our lives, whether we perceive those moments as good or bad.

The time has come for us. In Jesus, God has entered our world where we are born and die, work and play, love and dream. Let this Christmas time fill our lives with the knowledge that all our days are in God's hands. Since God joined us in our pain and disappointments, and knows our weakness and death, then let this Christmas time bring us strength, knowing that God's love is stronger than death, and God is able to bind up all our wounds. Since the time has come and God has rescued us from the sin that enslaves us—from the destruction we do to ourselves, to others, and to the creation itself—let this Christmas time fill us with the will to love and care for all. Yes, since the time has come and God has visited His people, let us join Mary and Joseph, the shepherds and angels, and all believers every-where this night to glorify and praise God. The time has come for all of that!

Rev. Ronald C. Starenko

A Time to Ponder

Luke 2:1

This is the hour for pondering, the place and time for pondering. What a won-derful word: "ponder." It means something like "meditate," but that sounds a little too active. "Ponder" comes from the Latin word *pondus*, meaning a "weight." "To ponder" means "to consider, to weigh, to hold in balance." "Mary treasured up all these things, pondering them in her heart" (Lk 2:19). Oh, such things she had to ponder! As I read the biblical account, I can picture something like the following.

THE DAY OF THE ANGEL

That's what she could have called it—the day she sat tending the fire, stirring the pot, when suddenly he stood in front of her. Strong and sure, with a voice that seemed to shake the foundations of her tiny house.

"Greetings, O favored one" (Lk 1:28) was his salutation. But she did not feel favored. Frightened, intimidated, yes—but not favored. She shook as though it were the coldest winter day. It was a bad dream. He must go away.

But he did not. Instead, he smiled. "Do not be afraid, Mary, for you have found favor with God. And behold, you will conceive in your womb and bear a son, and you shall call His name Jesus" (Lk 1:30–31).

Mary shivered again as she remembered. So strong was he. So bright. So glo-rious!

The angel sang of her son: "He will be great and will be called the Son of the Most High. And the Lord God will give to Him the throne of His father David, and He will reign over the house of Jacob forever, and of His kingdom there will be no end" (Lk 1:32–33).

She remembered the confusion. "How can this be? I have no husband." And the announcement of God's stirring within her. "For nothing will be impossible with God" (Lk 1:37).

She whispered, "Let it be to me according to Your word" (Lk 1:38). And then nothing. Just the fire and the simmering, blackened pot. Mary kept these things, pondering them in her heart.

Did She Ponder Elizabeth?

Old Elizabeth, her kinswoman, with folds under her eyes and chin, crow's-feet beside the deep brown eyes, and grey hair pulled back tight away from her face. When they met and Mary saw the puffy belly under the coarse robe, she clasped her hand over her mouth to keep from laughing. When Elizabeth saw this mere child stifling her giggles, she burst into a roar of laughter, and the two of them embraced with tears running down their cheeks. A girl barely a woman, and a six-month-pregnant senior citizen. "Oops," Elizabeth gasped. "He kicked! Little John kicked!" "Blessed are you among women, and blessed is the fruit of your womb!" (Lk 1:42). And they laughed again until Mary could only sing, "My soul magnifies the Lord, and my spirit rejoices in God my Savior" (Lk 1:46–47). For a high, holy hilarity is the height of praise.

The days spent with her elderly kinswoman were warm and peaceful as the child grew within her. Mary pondered.

Joseph: A Darker Memory

Her brows drew together as she remembered the shock and the anger and the confusion when she croaked out her story. Joseph was silent. Normally he was a quiet man, but now his silence was dark, almost dangerous. He left her in angry silence. But when he returned the next day, it was not with the rabbis. He smiled and held her and they were together. Something had happened. "Nothing will be impossible with God," the angel had said to her.

The Journey

She didn't know why she had to go. It would have been enough for Joseph to have gone, but he insisted. Later she would understand: it had to be in Bethlehem. But there was no room. The crowds and the confusion. She was pushed and jostled. The baby! Then there was a place for them, while others slept on street corners and alleyways. At last a cattle stall. She thinks of the smells, the animals, the manure; the sweetness of the hay; the heavy, assuring, sweaty odor of Joseph's body as she snuggled tight into him that night.

Then the Contractions Began

A twinge at first, then heavier, until her body felt like it would be torn apart. Joseph was standing over her, encouraging. Tears dripping off his cheeks into the hairs of his beard. "Yes, yes," he urged. And when it felt as though she could push no more, squeeze no stronger, a brittle cry in the night . . . and then the child in her arms.

She sang again, ever so weakly, "My soul magnifies the Lord, and my spirit rejoices in God my Savior." And then she slept.

Mary treasured all these things and pondered them in her heart.

SHE RECALLED THE SHEPHERDS

Funny little men. They were the ones her mother had warned her about. "Never speak to a shepherd," the woman had cautioned her. But now, they crowded into the smelly, dirty birthing room, pushing the cattle aside to glimpse at her little Yeshuah. Silent at first, mouths wide open as though they had never seen a baby before. But one of them spoke of angels—chanting, and lighting the shepherds' field with their presence. They didn't say much that night, but just sat on their haunches. She was so embarrassed. What did they want? They, too, were pondering in their own way until they rose, one by one, bowed low, and politely left. Once outside, she heard them hooting and yelping and running throughout the town like drunks. Mary and Joseph laughed again and held one another lightly, the baby safe between them.

Mary pondered. She treasured all these things and pondered them in her heart.

CAN WE JOIN HER IN PONDERING THIS NIGHT?

For that is what we are called to do at this hour. There will be time later for planning and applying the lessons, for studying the texts and trying to be rational about the whole thing. Except the essence of Christmas is not rational. God does not call His people to try to "figure out" Christmas Eve. Wait until Epiphany—that's when the Wise Men come. But even they weren't all that rational. They pondered all the way—following that elusive glowing in the heavens.

So tonight you are not called to be rational—just to praise! That's all. That's the goal of the Christmas Gospel—that, hearing this old story, it might move you, as it did the mother of the Lord, to sing sweetly, "My soul magnifies the Lord, and my spirit rejoices in God my Savior." For precious little of that magnifying and rejoicing takes place in this dark, cold world, where we believe that in our sinful musing and self-magnifying scheming we can get on and get ahead and make something of ourselves—as though God could not make something better.

What He makes of us, of course, is saints, beloved brothers and sisters of Mary who have the Christ Child nestled deep within ourselves by water and the Spirit. Ponder, too, what she will later ponder with her grey hair pulled tightly back and wrinkles creasing her pretty face.

PONDER THE DAY OF DARKNESS

When she stood beside not a manger of wood, but a grotesque cross of wood—looking up at her baby, whose face was drawn in pain, and who was wrapped not in swaddling cloths, but in nakedness. Ponder with her His love for her and for you, so great that it would drain from Him the final breath of life. Ponder that. Know that God so loved the world, and so loved you and me, that He gave His only-begotten Son, that whoever ponders and believes in Him will not perish, but have everlasting life.

And then, she took her firstborn son and wrapped Him in swaddling cloths and laid Him in a tomb.

But ponder, too, that He is risen—and so are you.

"Mary treasured up all these things, pondering them in her heart" (Lk 2:19). Sing with her tonight as you go out into a night not nearly as dark as when you entered this place.

"My soul magnifies the Lord, and my spirit rejoices in God my Savior" (Lk 1:46–47). And let the pondering people quietly say, "Amen."

Rev. Donald F. Hinchey

Overcome with Light!

John 1:1–4

Every Christmas we are overcome with lights. Stores try to capture our attention and interest with lights. Houses are decorated inside and out with lights of all descriptions. Lights add so much to our enjoyment this time of year, especially since the days are short and the nights are long. Unless we object to the glare—or to the usage of electricity—light is welcome and brings good cheer.

THE LIGHT OF JESUS CHRIST

What is it, then, that draws us here on Christmas Eve? Is it the desire for more light? Is it the softer, more gentle glow? No, we come to see the light of Jesus Christ. Tiring of the world's novelties and the busyness of this holy time, we long to hear again the message of Christ's birth—to see the light presented there.

The scene is familiar, committed to memory—it is distinctly one of lights. There, in a dimly lit stable, by the meager light of a lantern, we make out the image of a mother and her child—and the man, Joseph, who hovers over both in concern. We know the mother, Mary, and her child, the baby Jesus.

We know the visitors who will come that night. Shepherds leave their flocks to see the light. We know their story too. Under the light of the stars they had been watching their sheep when suddenly an angel appeared to them. The angel brings word of a special birth. At the end of this announcement a chorus of angels bursts upon the scene with "Glory to God in the highest, and on earth peace among those with whom He is pleased!" (Lk 2:14). This angelic chorus is prelude to the majesty awaiting them in the town below.

Light enhances the peaceful setting of Christmas. Yet it is not the light of the angel—nor the spectacular blast of thousands of angels—that God wants us to see. It is not the light of stars—or one star in particular—that God wants us to see. Neither is it the amber glow of lantern or campfire. It is the babe held in tender arms. The light is God's Son, Jesus Christ, who was ushered into the world to displace the darkness of sin and disgrace with the power of God's mercy and grace.

JESUS, THE CREATOR OF LIGHT

That light, Jesus Christ, is central to the story, but ironically it is the most easily ignored or excluded. Like a surgeon removing unwanted tissue or a photographer cropping an unwanted part of an image, Jesus is skillfully removed from the heart of His own celebration. The event or the season may be tolerably called Christmas, but the Christ is noticeably absent. The elements of angel and star may be prominent, but not the One whose birth they announced.

Plainly, Jesus is the light many do not wish to see. The glare is too intense. To say that Jesus is the light of the world would be to say that before Jesus came there was only darkness—and that without Him darkness rules, which is so very true. Before Jesus came, darkness reigned, physically and spiritually. The Bible makes it clear that Jesus was there before anything else was to bring about all things. The first command of God in creation was "Let there be light." The darkness disappeared. The Bible tells how Jesus shares in the very title of God. As John wrote in his Gospel, He was with God, before the face of God; He was the Word, He was the light; He was God. Elsewhere, John calls Jesus "the Alpha and the Omega, the first and the last, the beginning and the end" (Rev 22:13), descriptive terms given only to God. How many ways can it be expressed? There are some who will not see Jesus as the one who ushered in the dawn of creation and who literally dispelled the darkness, bringing forth this world and the cosmos as we know it.

JESUS DISPELS THE DARKNESS OF OUR LIVES

Then there is Jesus, the light who dispels the darkness of our spirit. This, too, is a point at which people avert their eyes. It might be even harder for some people to stand, for it presumes that there is a darkness in our own lives that needs to be dispelled. That also is true. Moved by the Holy Spirit, Zechariah prophesied that Jesus would be the one who would come "to [redeem] His people . . . to show the mercy promised to our fathers and to remember His holy covenant . . . that we, being delivered from the hand of our enemies, might serve Him without fear, in holiness and righteousness before Him all our days" (Lk 1:68–75).

To know Jesus is to have our lives changed. Any light we claim to have is artificial—any goodness, any knowledge, any wisdom, anything—does not compare to the light God shines into our life through Jesus Christ. Through Jesus we begin to see what we otherwise would not recognize: that we fall woefully short of God's glory. Jesus stated this clearly when He said to a skeptical Nicodemus:

> This is the judgment: the light has come into the world, and people loved the darkness rather than the light because their deeds were evil. For everyone who does wicked things hates the light and does not come to the light, lest his deeds should be exposed. But whoever does what is true comes to the light, so that it may be clearly seen that his deeds have been carried out in God. (Jn 3:19–21)

At Christmas, God the Father brought the light into the world of darkness. Christmas is fully God's work to bring the world out of darkness into His marvelous light; in so doing, He brought us peace. Where there is darkness, there is doubt, uncertainty, and fear. Jesus came to bring light. Jesus spoke the truth about our natural condition, but more important, He spoke of God's love for us and His desire to save His people from their sins. Jesus displayed that love in all He said and did.

Although He was truly God, Jesus entered into the darkness of our human life. God's light fully penetrated the darkness of the world and was not overcome by it. He knew the depths of human depravity, but He walked among it—the pure amid the impure. He allowed Himself to share in the greatest depths of our human woe to bring about something spectacular. Jesus entered into death itself, allowing His human life to be extinguished, because only in this way would He fully breach the darkness and destroy that which otherwise would engulf us forever. Even in death, the light prevailed. His resurrection on Easter morning drove out the darkness of sin and dispersed the gloom of death. The wages of sin is death, but Jesus has paid the perfect price. Therefore, in Jesus' name and for His sake, God grants us the gift of eternal life.

By God's grace, the light of Christ has come to shine on our life. It sparkles in the water of Baptism, which works faith in us and cleanses us of sin. It shines brightly in our life, bringing joy, causing doubt and deceit to melt into the shadows. The light of Christ releases us from the realm of satanic power and brings clarity to an otherwise distorted and desperate world. The light of Christ shines on our path and guides our way in His righteousness. By this light our days are blessed, and we rejoice in the covenant proclaimed in His name.

Enjoy the lights that abound in this season, if you will, but bask in the light that God provides through His Son, the light who overwhelms us with life and by the grace of God illumines our day.

Rev. Eric L. Zacharias

Christmas Candlelight
or Christmas Dawn

The Sparkle of Light

John 1:4–5

In early Christian times, long before hydroelectric or nuclear power plants existed, a blessing was said as the household lamps were lighted. As the spark ignited the wick, the lamplighter would say, "Praise God, who sends us the light of heaven."[18]

That, in a nutshell, is the intention of the candlelight service. It is to praise God, who indeed has sent us the light of heaven—Jesus Christ, who has become the light of the world. In the calm glitter of a quiet moment, we discover the sparkle of His light. And we sense that the darkness can no longer frighten us or cause us pain.

Cultures the world over consider light to be a sign of good, of knowledge. By contrast, darkness connotes evil and lack of knowledge. "Let light shine and darkness be banished forever!" we might shout. Let the brightness of Christ illumine the world this night and every night so that no one need ever crouch in fear again.

There is a special quality in this light we know as the Christ of Christmas. It is what the evangelist John identified as inherent in Jesus alone. "In Him," he writes, "was life, and the life was the light of men" (Jn 1:4).

When the October 17, 1989, Loma Prieta earthquake struck the San Francisco Bay Area, the Santa Clara Valley rocked furiously, and the neighborhood in San Jose where Lois and I lived was without light for over four hours. That was nothing compared to those who went without electricity for weeks, but it was long enough to remind us that in light is life, and in uncertain darkness the threat of death lurks. We had to borrow a neighbor's camp light to brighten our dismal darkness that autumn evening.

God, compassionately viewing His creation, saw humanity cowering in the gloom of sin. He saw us tumbling to our deaths in the moral and spiritual darkness that engulfed us. He who once said, "Let there be light" (Gen 1:3) as the universe was created, echoed that command anew to bring to this planet a Light more powerful than the sun. It was to be His Son, in whom indeed there would be life—life that He would live; life meant for now, and a life that would go on forever. "I am the way, and the truth, and the life," He said. "No one comes to the Father except through Me" (Jn 14:6). Because of Him, we need stumble in the darkness no longer. Jesus lights the way.

---

18 Rumer Godden in *The Book of Christmas* (Pleasantville, NY: Reader's Digest, 1973), 39.

Thus we focus on Bethlehem and that tiny infant who illumined the whole world with a love that never pales. We see the Virgin tenderly holding her child, and Joseph keeping a watchful eye in that cramped stable, filled as it must have been with barnyard animals, their pungent aromas mixed with the smell of straw, the cooing of the doves augmented by the occasional braying of a donkey and bleating of a sheep. The shepherds arrive with the excitement of children to marvel at what the angels had said and to tell their wondrous story of hearing the heavenly hosts praising God and revealing the birth of the Messiah. Through Bethlehem's dark fields they stumbled toward the one glowing light, that baby called Jesus, whom Isaiah named Immanuel, "God with us."

There in that manger, the battle between light and dark was joined, the war between life and death encountered. Isaiah foretold centuries before, "The people who walked in darkness have seen a great light; those who dwelt in a land of deep darkness, on them has light shined" (Is 9:2). "For to us a child is born, to us a son is given; and the government shall be upon His shoulder, and His name shall be called Wonderful Counselor, Mighty God, Everlasting Father, Prince of Peace" (v. 6), concluded the prophet. But Jesus Himself put it more simply, "I am the light of the world. Whoever follows Me will not walk in darkness, but will have the light of life" (Jn 8:12). He said at another time, "The light is among you for a little while longer. Walk while you have the light, lest darkness overtake you. . . . While you have the light, believe in the light, that you may become sons of light" (Jn 12:35–36).

Thus that tiny glitter in the crib in the inn's stable became more than a glowing ember—a consuming fire, filled with warmth and brightness and light, igniting the whole world, banishing the darkness and giving sparkle to life.

Seven hundred years before Joseph led Mary along the rocky path to Bethlehem, Israel was told that a virgin would give birth to a unique child who would save humanity from its sins. Isaiah spoke of a bridge that would span from God's heaven into our sinful world. This virgin-born child was no myth, but a light to shrink the darkness. And what a flame He has been to us ever since; what a light to dispel the night of fear!

An agile man trudged through the crisp Saxon snow one Christmas Eve more than 450 years ago thinking this very thought, when he caught a sparkle out of the corner of his eye that captured his imagination. He stopped in his tracks and trained his eyes upon a small tree covered with glittering snow that seemed like diamond dust in the bright light of the moon. With his axe, he chopped down the small fir and carried it to his home in the Black Cloister of Wittenberg. His children were startled to see their father drag a tree into the house. Katie, his good wife, was amazed to see him set it up in the parlor. The man rummaged in a cabinet for a small box of candles and placed them carefully on the branches, melting wax underneath to hold them in place. Before long the room took on an unusual glow and the first Christmas tree was inaugurated.

Martin Luther pointed to the candles and told his children that they are reminders of the Light of the world—Jesus Christ—and the branches, still green in the midst of winter, are reminders of the eternal life Jesus gives to those who believe.[19] One can imagine the reformer instructing his youngsters how the light of Jesus dispels the darkness of sin.

Ever since, around the world trees have been brought indoors from the forests and made to shimmer with candles and electric lights in an effort to recall the light Christ brings to our lives, dispelling the darkness of sin and doubt, heartache and sorrow.

It is impossible for me to know the deep fears and earnest pains that afflict your soul, but God knows. You may be troubled by an insidious disease or have suffered loss or endured an unpleasant encounter. But He who is light and life comes with the brilliance of His love and the miracle of His forgiveness. Shimmering in the redness of wine, He comes. In the whiteness of a wafer of bread, He offers you Himself to dispel your darkness and give greater brilliance to your faith. He comes that you may have life, and have it abundantly (Jn 10:10). He comes in Word and Sacrament to make of your heart a Bethlehem stable.

Jesus came as light and burned brightly, giving life to those who followed Him; yet death stalked Him as it does us all. But the shadow of Good Friday did not conceal the brightness long. With the rising of the sun on Easter, the Son of God also arose. His luminous message took on an aura never seen before, and still it glitters, scattering the darkness and deepening our joy.

May the light of Jesus bring life to you this Christmas. May His sparkle gleam within your soul, and may the devilish darkness that threatens us be banished by the true light that never fades.

In a candlelight service the small candle each parishioner holds brings a small glow. But when our whole congregation holds high the little torches, the sanctuary sparkles brightly. Thus, Christians, God has turned on the light. Lift it high!

Rev. Richard Andersen

---

19 Godden, *Book of Christmas*, 67.

The Angel's Message
Luke 2:1–20 (especially vv. 9–14)

(Propose that the stanzas be sung by a solo male voice until the last stanza, when all are invited to join in [*LSB* 358].)

[This sermon can be paired with the Christmas Day sermon "The Shepherd's Response" on pp. 156–59.—Ed.]

It is Christmas Eve. The worship at church is over. The family is gathered in the living room. Father has written a new Christmas song for his wife and children. He sings it softly:

> "From heav'n above to earth I come
> To bear good news to ev'ry home;
> Glad tidings of great joy I bring
> To all the world and gladly sing. (*LSB* 358:1)

The words were new, but the children recognize the melody. It was part of a singing game they knew. A young man would sing:

> Good news from far above I bring
> Glad tidings for you all I sing.
> I bring so much you'd like to know,
> Much more than I shall tell you, though.

Then the young man would propose a riddle to one of the girls. If she could not solve the riddle, she had to forfeit the wreath she wore as a headdress.

But the father had much more in mind than a singing game. He wished for the family to use a familiar melody to sing about a most precious event. He writes fourteen more stanzas to share the message. Eight of them are to be sung on Christmas Eve and six of them on Christmas morning. The second stanza gets right to the heart of the matter:

> "To you this night is born a child
> Of Mary, chosen virgin mild;
> This little child of lowly birth
> Shall be the joy of all the earth. (*LSB* 358:2)

The father knows the deep significance of this birth. He knows it for himself. He knows it for his family. He knows it for the Church.

He knows that of himself, life would be quite joyless because of what by nature went through his mind, because of what came out of his mouth, because of some of the deeds that he did. They were wrong. They were evil. They were hurtful.

He knows that what is true for him is also true for his family. He has watched them. He has listened to them. He knows there are too many times when they have no joy, and they have robbed others of joy. But this is the night when joy is restored.

> "This is the Christ, our God Most High,
> Who hears your sad and bitter cry;
> He will Himself your Savior be
> From all your sins to set you free. (*LSB* 358:3)

The amazing truth the father wishes his family to know is that this is not an afterthought of God. Nor is it one thought among many. This is God's plan. It has been the promised plan for a very long time. He sings:

> "He will on you the gifts bestow
> Prepared by God for all below,
> That in His kingdom, bright and fair,
> You may with us His glory share. (*LSB* 358:4)

"Be comforted, my dear ones," the father intones. No matter how joyless, no matter how distressing, no matter how empty life may have become, God has not forgotten you. He has not forsaken you. God is faithful. He keeps His promises. Listen to the message of the angels:

> "These are the signs that you shall mark:
> The swaddling clothes and manger dark.
> There you will find the infant laid
> By whom the heav'ns and earth were made." (*LSB* 358:5)

Then the father, the venerable Dr. Martin Luther, encourages his family to respond with the shepherds of long ago. He had undoubtedly spent time in the open fields, wondering what he would have done had the angels come to him. He could understand their sense of unworthiness, their amazement and surprise. He could understand their desire to confirm what had been told them. So, he would sing:

> How glad we'll be to find it so!
> Then with the shepherds let us go
> To see what God for us has done
> In sending us His own dear Son.
>
> Come here, my friends, lift up your eyes
> And see what in the manger lies.
> Who is this child, so young and fair?
> It is the Christ Child lying there. (*LSB* 358:6–7)

What the family, with the shepherds, and with the whole Church saw was none other than the Son of God. The Son of God, born of Mary. The Son of God, laid in a manger. The Son of God born to free the world and us from sin's slavery. The Son of God, born to love us infinitely and without qualification.

Sing with Dr. Luther and his family:

Ah, dearest Jesus, holy Child,
Prepare a bed, soft, undefiled,
A quiet chamber, set apart
For You to dwell within my heart. (*LSB* 358:13)

Rev. Vernon D. Gundermann

Christmas Day

Among Us

John 1:1–14

For me—perhaps for you too—worship on Christmas Day reaches a depth of meaning that is hard to come by on Christmas Eve. To be sure, Christmas Eve is an emotional moment with an impact on people no one would want to give up—the lights, the gifts, the tree, the family togetherness, the childhood memories, the anticipation. That's meaningful to me, indeed to all of us.

When we reach Christmas Day, however, most of that is over. Here we are, fewer in number (for that reason, some churches don't have Christmas Day services). The hype is gone, the Christmas tree looks so different in the daylight, and the world around us has shut down. And that's an advantage for us, I think. We are not caught up in the hectic countdown that started weeks ago; we are not distracted by the secular approach to Christmas; we are able to focus on something we perhaps could not have last night. We are better prepared today to deal with the central affirmation of the Christian faith, which probably is also the central offense of the faith, namely, that "the Word became flesh and dwelt among us" (Jn 1:14).

In some ways, this is almost the reverse of what we were about last night. Christmas can very easily become an escape from the world as we know it—a flight into unreality, I would call it. By means of all the traditions and symbols and activity we can translate ourselves into a world that is beautiful and fanciful, a world of dreams and emotions; a happy, harmonious world, even if it lasts only for a few hours. We are, then, in the world of fantasy, while the truest meaning of Christmas has to do with the world of the flesh.

Christians—and other people for that matter—have always had a problem with the flesh, in this case, with the humanity of Jesus. Notice how quick we are to defend the divinity of our Lord, often at the expense of His humanity. The creedal statement, "Jesus is Lord," forms on our lips easier than the assertion, "Jesus is our brother." The truth is that we are more comfortable with a Jesus who promises us everlasting life, a heavenly home, an escape from a world that is filled with sin and pain—a Jesus who is not really part of our blood and sweat and tears.

We could define the original sin described in the story of Adam and Eve as a refusal to be human, wanting to be like God. To be human means to be in this world, to live in dependence upon God, to be humane to one another—in other words, to be servants rather than lords. To be human is to be content to be a creature. To be human in this now-fallen world means to be willing to suffer for the sake of Christ and to be willing to suffer for others in order to share Christ's love. Yes,

I believe we have a problem with being human. It is a gift often unaffirmed, if not despised.

It seems to me that to affirm truly our humanity is to profess that we have been made and redeemed by God, and He is among us. "The Word became flesh and dwelt among us." Those who had a problem with Jesus opposed Him because He said that God was at work in and through Him. That was offensive to those who wanted to keep God at arm's length, preferably back in heaven. Let God rule from the heavens with judgments against the wicked and blessings for the good. It would be a scandal for God to come among us as a weak human, to associate even with the worst sinners, for then we would be compelled to affirm our humanity, to recognize all people equally as God's creatures and objects of His love. It would mean that we worship a God of grace and forgiveness right here in the midst of humans called to be the body of Christ, right here in a common meal shared by those in Christ.

That's what Christmas is all about—God among us. That is what informs the meaning of Jesus' death and resurrection—that He is God manifest in the flesh. Without the incarnation, there is no Gospel to hear or tell. But John begins his Gospel by immediately affirming that the Logos, the God who created all things in the beginning, now joins His creation by means of the flesh, the humanity of Jesus. The implications are mind-blowing as well as life-changing.

Hear it clearly: the love of God is an incarnate love; a love our God lived out in flesh and blood. It is among us; it is here, a reality. Love is not an emotion floating around. It is present in Jesus, who reached out to people—even unlovable people. He drew near to sinners; He touched people who were hurting. He touched them and brought them the forgiveness of God. That love of God has touched us and is in us, in you and me. As the Church, as God's redeemed and reclaimed humanity, we bring to the world an acceptance and an affirmation that is the very presence of God. Make no mistake about it: the Word is working in us flesh-and-blood people so that others will know God is among us.

God is among us—in the world as it really is, despite the pride and greed, the vanity and ambition, the inhumanity and racial hatred. He is with us despite the world's strife, ruthless violence, and senseless deaths. He came to this world where the innocent are crushed, where the weak are tossed aside.

God is among us on the cross. From the time Jesus was born, His life was directed toward saving us. He is among us, out of the tomb, let loose in the world. He is among us—the Word made flesh in real people like you and me, in an ordinary-looking Meal that celebrates the saving death of the Incarnate One. He is among us for all time and eternity.

Wouldn't you agree that this is the word we need today, at a time when we are losing our humanity and our souls in the process? Wouldn't you agree that there would be no hope for us unless God had became a human being, united God's Spirit with our spirits, and destined us to have God's life in our bodies? Wouldn't you agree that Christmas means our lives are worth living, and the world in which we live is worth saving?

Here is the glory of God. Here is where grace and truth are found: in the lowly One who is born of Mary, who identifies with sinners, who blesses ordinary things, who calls us to be His servants. Not to see that glory of God is to miss out on Christmas, no matter what we do on Christmas Eve or Christmas Day. To see, with John and all God's people through the centuries, the true glory of Christmas is to recognize that God is among us in the person of Jesus, now and forever.

Rev. Ronald C. Starenko

It's a Boy!

Luke 2:7

It's a boy! Mary had a baby! It's a boy! Can you imagine Joseph's joy? I shall always remember the great joy God gave me each time I became a father. You have seen it, too, haven't you? You grandparents have gotten that phone call—"It's a boy! Everyone is doing fine!"

We have added so much decoration and glitter and fuss and bother to Christmas that the basic story easily gets lost. It's a boy! While Mary and Joseph knew this Son was special, at the same time they celebrated: It's a boy! Mother and baby are doing fine! When God blesses us with the miracle of birth, we want to know three things:

First: Is it a boy or a girl?

Second: How is the mother doing?

Third: Is the baby healthy?

St. Luke answers these basic questions concerning Jesus' birth in our text. Inspired by the Holy Spirit, he did his homework before he wrote his Gospel. Many people believe Luke talked directly to Mary and had her direct testimony.

First Question: Is It a Boy or a Girl?

"[Mary] gave birth to her firstborn son" (Lk 2:7). It's a boy! More than that, He is her first child. Firstborn sons are important to Jewish families. We remember that the firstborn sons in Egyptian families died when Moses led the people of Israel out of Egypt. After that, all the firstborn sons of Israel belonged to God, but they could be bought back through the sacrifice of a lamb at the temple. A firstborn son received an inheritance twice that of any of his brothers. It's a boy! A firstborn son! Many commentators believe that Luke's choice of the word *firstborn* suggests that Mary had more children. We can read in the Gospels about Jesus' brothers and sisters.

SECOND QUESTION: HOW IS THE MOTHER DOING?

"[Mary] wrapped Him in swaddling cloths and laid Him in a manger" (v. 7). Mother Mary is doing fine. She is up on her feet. That same night she received visitors, the shepherds. Luke tells us that after the shepherds left, "Mary treasured up all these things, pondering them in her heart" (Lk 2:19). A woman in pain does not concern herself with singing angels and smelly shepherds. Mother Mary is doing fine. It's a boy! Mary cared for Him.

THIRD QUESTION: IS THE BABY HEALTHY?

"[Mary] wrapped Him in swaddling cloths and laid Him in a manger" (v. 7). The word that Luke uses for "gave birth" implies the live birth of a healthy child. Had baby Jesus been sick, Mary would not have put Him in a feedbox. Mary would have cradled Him in her arms and rocked Him and prayed for Him and kept Him warm. Had baby Jesus been sickly, Joseph would have gone for help. Baby Jesus is doing fine. Thank you for asking.

Jesus' heavenly Father and the Holy Spirit inspired Luke to answer the first three questions we ask at every birth: It's a boy. Mother Mary is doing fine. Baby Jesus is healthy. So what? What does this have to do with us? Millions of healthy firstborn sons have been born to healthy women. Why do we make such a fuss over this one birth two thousand years ago? Let's look at those three answers again.

FIRST: IT'S A BOY!

A human baby boy! We call today the Nativity of our Lord. The Word became flesh. God Himself became a human being. He is one of us! Consider just what that means.

When a basketball coach wants to send a new player into the game, he looks to his own bench. He does not send one of his opposing coach's players into the game. It is the same way with God the Father. When He needed a substitute to die for our sins, He sent neither a lamb nor a dog nor a cockroach. He sent a human like us. Jesus could pay for our sins because He was born a human being. It's a boy!

You and I needed someone to substitute for us. Just look at what we have done to Christmas. Do we worship the Lord of Bethlehem? Or do we worship at Hudsons, at Sears, at Lord & Taylor? Is our Christmas full of the Holy Spirit, who came to us in our Baptism? Or is it mostly some undefined and nebulous "spirit of Christmas"? Is your heart full of angel songs, or does your Christmas cheer come out of a bottle? Do we hear sweet voices of children singing "Mary had a baby"? Or are our homes full of the zap, zing, bing, bong of video games? O Lord, forgive us our Christmases!

We need a substitute to pay the price of our corrupted Christmases. And we have a substitute worthy and willing to come for us. It's a boy!

SECOND: MOTHER MARY IS DOING FINE

Jesus was born into a human family. Like you, Jesus had a mother and father and brothers and sisters. He knows from firsthand experience what it is to have parents who do not completely understand Him. He knows from firsthand experience what it is to have squabbling brothers and sisters. He knows from firsthand experience what it is to have siblings who doubt Him and who desert Him when He is hurting. Mother Mary had to be healthy to give Jesus a normal human family. She and Joseph were there to teach Him basic Jewish family values. Mother Mary is doing fine.

We are blessed because Mary was blessed. Jesus was born to die for us. A sword pierced Mary's heart when Jesus died on the cross. Jesus also was born to live for us. Jesus lived a perfect life for you in a family much like yours. In order for His death in your place to mean anything, He had to live a perfect life for you. Jesus lived perfectly for you in the face of all the same temptations that come to you. Mother Mary was part of God's plan to make possible Jesus' perfect life for you. Mother Mary is doing fine. Thank you for asking.

THIRD: BABY JESUS IS HEALTHY

He had to be healthy. Look at what He faced as He grew up: less than two years after His birth, He and His parents became nighttime fugitives. The Gaza Strip is not a healthy place for travelers today. The Gaza Strip was not safe for the fleeing holy family either. Life as the son of a carpenter in the hills of Nazareth was as hard as life in the coal-mining hills of Kentucky is today. Jesus spent weeks alone in the desert. He served in a preaching and teaching ministry on the road. He organized a traveling seminary for His followers. All this is hard work. Then His body and spirit bore the mockery of crowds, the agony in the garden, the beatings, the scourging, the thorns, the cross. Only a strong and healthy body could carry all this for you.

Baby Jesus is healthy. He grew up to be a strong and healthy man. He lived perfectly for you. He died perfectly for you. His Father in heaven said, "This is My beloved Son, with whom I am well pleased" (Mt 3:17). It is as though the Father were saying, "It's a boy! I am so proud of what He is doing. I shall raise Him from the dead!"

Now Jesus sits on the throne in heaven with a resurrected and perfect body. Soon you and I also shall be standing before Him with perfect bodies. Our sins are forgiven. Our Christmases are forgiven. Jesus is still a human. He still knows the troubles you have. He knows and prays for you. He can pray for you because He has been here. He has lived among us. It's a boy!

Today part of our world says: "Ho! Ho! Ho!" Another part of the world says: "Bah! Humbug!" You and I have a different message to share: "Look! Look! Look! It's a boy!"

Rev. Warren E. Messmann

Christmas Eucharist Sermon

A Perfect Christmas

Titus 2:11–14

Some years ago, at a Christmas Eve service, things were perfect. The congregation was celebrating Christmas in their new sanctuary for the first time. The church was beautiful. The wall behind the altar had been designed to hold many poinsettias—and they were beautiful.

A young boy had flawlessly sung the first stanza of "Once in Royal David's City." The vocal and instrumental musicians were on the same page, the same chord. Their tone, energy, and volume were sensitive and beautiful. The liturgy was engaging, so that those who had not been to church for a long time and those who had been often were drawn together and blended with the worshipers of the Christ Child through the ages. The burning candles cast embracing and enhancing light on the walls and on the faces of the worshipers. The preacher was focused, catching the attention of both the easily bored and the eagerly attentive.

In the congregation were children snuggled close to their parents, feeling secure and safe and loved; dating couples, hopeful that their new friend would be someone special; engaged couples, planning their wedding and their future; married couples, who had worked through the struggles of their relationship and were feeling confident and secure; older parents, some, singled by the death of their spouses, accompanied by their adult children and feeling grateful and blessed, many who felt good about the gifts they had received and even better about the gifts they had given.

For many it seemed a perfect Christmas.

Then, as the liturgy for Holy Communion began, the platform for the poinsettias wobbled. Suddenly, with a resounding crash, the poinsettias fell. Clay pots broke loudly. Dirt and tangled plants spewed everywhere. It was a mess.

For some, the perfect Christmas had been shattered. But for most, Christmas was perfected in the sharing of the bread and the wine amid broken pots. The pots made it clear that our world is broken, but into this brokenness Christ came. And that in the midst of the desperate efforts for a perfect Christmas, it was only in the brokenness that Christmas became perfect.

Christ did not come into a perfect world. It was a broken one. Some of the breaking was loud and messy with dirt and twisted plants everywhere. Still, He came. He came so fragile, so breakable. He came to be broken on the cross. Not a bone of His was broken when they nailed Him there, but He was broken away from God, separated from His Father as He suffered hell in our place. He took the punishment for our sins upon Himself. He died for us. But God did not leave Him in the grave. God raised Him from the dead and placed Him on a throne at His right hand to rule His kingdom.

Because Jesus was broken on the cross for our sins and healed again in blessed reunion with the Father, He can heal our brokenness by forgiving our sins and uniting us with Himself. That is why He was born. He came to assure us that despite how desperately we want a perfect Christmas, no Christmas can be perfect until our brokenness is healed in Him.

Come to the meal that is of Christ. He gives us His broken body so our brokenness can be healed. Come to this Holy Meal that takes away all of our broken and scattered messes with the touch of His great love. He does not reject or forsake us in our brokenness. He joins us and He heals us.

Are you having a perfect Christmas? Probably not. Something may have fallen off your own wall. Someone may have disappointed you. It is okay. You are still having a Christmas that is perfect because Christ has come into our broken world. He allows us to say this night, and every Christmas—without reference to gifts or family or events—that in Christ we are having a perfect Christmas.

Rev. Vernon D. Gundermann

The Shepherds' Response

Luke 2:1–20 (especially vv. 15–20)

(Propose that the stanzas be sung by a solo male voice until the last stanza, when all are invited to join in [*LSB* 358].)

[This sermon can be paired with the Christmas Eve sermon "The Angel's Message" on pp. 145–47.—Ed.]

It is Christmas Day! What a wonderful day! May our Lord bless you richly on this Christmas Day.

It is not surprising if some of you are a little tired. There is so much that happens on Christmas Eve. There are all of those last-minute details to finish—gifts to purchase and wrap, food to prepare, even possibly last-minute travel to arrange. To celebrate Christmas Eve more often than not takes a lot of energy.

Besides that, for many of you Christmas Eve included worship, and if you went to the later candlelight service, it was after midnight when you left here. It is no wonder some of us are a little tired.

I can only imagine how many were exhausted on that first Christmas Day. Mary and Joseph were certainly exhausted. The shepherds were certainly tired. They probably had no rest at all.

Still, Christmas Day must have been exciting for them. Nothing would ever be the same again! Christ, the Savior, was born!

CELEBRATE THE SAVIOR'S BIRTH THROUGH SONG

So we come to worship this day probably a little tired, yet also excited, for we have come still again to celebrate the very good news that "Christ, the Savior, is born!" (*LSB* 363:2).

So, how might we celebrate this Christmas Day? Let's continue what we started last evening, at our candlelight liturgies. A focal point for our worship was Dr. Martin Luther's much-loved hymn, "From Heaven above to Earth I Come." He had written that hymn for his family's Christmas celebration. The hymn has fifteen stanzas, believe it or not, and is based on a singing game that young people played in his day.

We sang eight of those stanzas last evening. They centered on the angel's message to the shepherds. Many of them were sung by a solo voice. We have six stanzas to sing this morning. They are called "The Shepherds' Response," and are our response as well. Although a little tired, we are filled with joy, and we sing:

> Welcome to earth, O noble Guest,
> Through whom the sinful world is blest!
> You came to share my misery
> That You might share Your joy with me. (*LSB* 358:8)

Welcome! How can we appropriately welcome to our world and our lives the very Son of God? How do we respond to one who with good cause might have chosen to ignore us? Oh, I know. We feel fairly significant this morning. We gave some gifts that came from our heart to those we love. We received gifts that called for much thought and were just right.

Still, we know ourselves. We are aware of how amazing God's love is. He loves us! "Welcome to earth, O noble Guest!" Welcome to our world! Welcome to our lives!

It is amazing! It is amazing that He loves us! It is amazing the form His love took. He who created everything became so small. It fascinates children and amazes adults. We sing:

> Ah, Lord, though You created all,
> How weak You are, so poor and small,
> That You should choose to lay Your head
> Where lowing cattle lately fed! (*LSB* 358:9)

THE GIVER OF ALL GIFTS IS THE GIFT HIMSELF

Dr. Luther penned two stanzas that compare what Jesus was certainly worthy of and what He chose for Himself. Dr. Luther knew his world as we know ours. When you really want to show honor to someone so worthy, you give them the very best, from elegant clothes to precious jewels.

What is most impressive is what one who is entitled to so much chooses for himself. The God who created everything and who is entitled to anything chooses things that are nothing for Himself. I love the way Dr. Luther said this, and I imagine you do too. Please sing:

> Were earth a thousand times as fair
> And set with gold and jewels rare,
> It would be far too poor and small
> A cradle for the Lord of all.
>
> Instead of soft and silken stuff
> You have but hay and straw so rough
> On which as King, so rich and great,
> To be enthroned in royal state. (*LSB* 358:10–11)

So, how do we respond? How do we, a little tired but filled with gratitude and joy, respond? How do we, who know we deserve no gift at all (maybe only a piece of coal), respond to having the greatest gift of all? How do we, who have messed up most gifts we have received in the past, who have messed up this gift way too often, respond when the Giver of all gifts is Himself the gift?

How do we respond when we know so much? We know at least three things that shape our response. We know that we will keep on messing up this wonderful gift. We know we will undervalue it, we will ignore it, and we will abuse it.

We know that as humble as Christ has chosen to come into our world, He will, for our sake, be humbled even more. He will live among sinful people and will be abandoned by sinful disciples. He will be denied justice by sinful government officials and rejected by sinful church leaders. He will be put to death by sinful executioners and buried by crushed followers.

We also know that He will rise from the grave for you and me. And in His resurrection He will make sure we receive so much more than we deserve. He promises to be with us every day of our lives with the fullness of His love and grace.

To Sing with the Angels

Then, when life is ended, while we deserve an eternal bed of straw and hay, He promises to dress us in the royal robes of righteousness and enthrone us at the royal banquet table—of which there will be no end.

Dr. Luther's great hymn concludes with two stanzas that give voice to a response that we pray, with the angel hosts, will go on and on. Please stand to sing:

> My heart for very joy must leap;
> My lips no more can silence keep.
> I, too, must sing with joyful tongue
> That sweetest ancient cradlesong:
>
> Glory to God in highest heav'n,
> Who unto us His Son has giv'n!
> While angels sing with pious mirth
> A glad new year to all the earth. (*LSB* 358:14–15)

Rev. Vernon D. Gundermann

The Banner of Christ Is Lifted High

Isaiah 62:10–12

The day of Christmas has arrived. Here in our sanctuary we gather and sing the beautiful hymns of this season. "Silent Night" has led us into choruses of "Joy to the World!" with rounds of "Alleluias!" echoing around and through this church. Truly, God has gathered us to celebrate the gift of His Son, Jesus, whose birth will bring us joy and eternal peace.

At home, however, a different scene may await us. According to custom, we may have ceremoniously opened gifts. Following our worship we will return home and survey the scene. The joy and satisfaction we experienced at church will follow us home, but once there, things may transform. Our joy may simply be having made it through another Christmas. The shopping is complete, the schedule of events fulfilled. There are items probably yet on the agenda—places to go, people to see, things to do—but by and large you and I may be looking forward to a time when we can settle down and rest.

The battle has been won. We might have suffered loss on one front or another, but we have managed to come out somewhat victorious. Now there can be peace. Later on we will continue to evaluate things, calculating the wins and the losses and determining the actual "success" of this holiday season. Were there casualties? Did tempers flair? Is the damage severe or minimal? How big a hit was this—for the kids, for the parents, for the bank account? That is the human side of the celebration of Christmas.

God's Great Gift of Jesus

We often have placed too much on the "things" that surround the day of Jesus' birth. If our expectations have been placed on that side of the ledger, then there is little wonder we fall all over ourselves as the day arrives. God brought about this day to focus on the gift that He provides. Front and center is Jesus Christ, who was sent to speak God's peace and to deliver us from our sins.

If your temper did flare along the way or if you sinned in a big way, do you believe that God is able and willing to forgive you? If you were caught in a battle of wills, do you believe that God is available to work with you to bring about His will in your life? If you were hurt or frustrated—or passed that on to others—do you believe that God can make things right or set things in the proper direction? If you have suffered trials, temptation, or exceptional burdens, do you believe that God will lift that burden from your shoulders and give you strength and healing? If you expected much or carried the weight of another's expectation, do you believe that God can give you a spirit of contentment and peace? God is able and willing to do exactly these things and more. This day He calls you forward to receive these gifts, which only come from Him.

We battle many things in life, and frankly, it is unrealistic to think that these things suddenly disappear in the magical season of Christmas. As many of you know, the battles only intensify. And few things seem to be settled or properly resolved. That does not take away from what God is proclaiming through His Word, nor does it nullify or weaken the message of Jesus Christ.

Christmas Is a Battlefield

In fact, the arrival of Jesus Christ is the greatest reality God wants us to see. Christmas is a battlefield, not simply as we find it in our experience (in the mall, at the bank, or in our homes). Christmas is a point in history where God confronted evil. From the first day that Satan rebelled against God, a war was underway for the crown of God's creation—the heart of man. Sadly, we know all too well the victory that sin has had in our own life and the pain that echoes through creation itself. We have experienced the war that wages from within—the desire to sin, to assert ourselves at the expense of others, to have our own way. The world has suffered at the hands of others who desire to do the same.

In history God lifted up His people, calling them to look up and to move forward, because salvation from sin and every evil would be supplied by God Himself. In the Bible we see God calling His people forth in faith, leading them out of slavery into a land they would have as their own. We find that time and again, God is there not merely to rally the troops, but to lead the charge, fight the fight, engage and disarm the enemy, and lead His people forward in joyous victory. God announced through His prophet Isaiah a wonderful proclamation:

Go through, go through the gates; prepare the way for the people; build up, build up the highway; clear it of stones; lift up a signal over the peoples. (Is 62:10)

The people were aware of their sins. Are you? They had suffered for their misplaced loyalties and their wandering faith. Have you? They knew how their ancestors felt as helpless nobodies, and they longed for the time when God would gather them together, as He had done in the past. Do you have that longing?

They welcomed the words of their Lord. And you do too. They longed for the coming of their Lord. And you do too. They looked for the banner that would rally them as a nation and move them forward as a people. And you do too.

The banner is Jesus Christ, the one whom God lifted up for His people to see. The heavens reverberated with the joyous celebration on the hills as angels passed on the message to the toughened troop of shepherds gathered in the watching of sheep outside the town of Bethlehem.

God lifted up His banner for the world to see, sending the star that would lead the Wise Men from a great distance over treacherous terrain, that they, too, would have word that God's promise of a great King had come.

God lifted up His Son, Jesus, who would engage the devil on every front. The devil, who loves to twist the truth, held not an inch against He who is the truth. Jesus spoke with amazing authority and power. The devil, whose skill is seen in the manipulation and destruction of human lives, was no match against Him who held all lives in His hand—people were delivered from sickness, demonic-possession, and even from death itself.

One day Satan suddenly found all things coming his way. He soon found Jesus in the hands of evil men. He found Jesus bound and condemned as an evil man, sent on His way to the accursed death on a cross. No doubt, it was a delightful moment for the devil when he saw the banner of Christ lifted high—a spectacle of failure if ever there was one!

Then Satan saw all come undone. As Jesus was lifted high Satan realized the fulfillment of Jesus' words. To His followers Jesus had said, "Now is the judgment of this world; now will the ruler of this world be cast out. And I, when I am lifted up from the earth, will draw all people to Myself" (Jn 12:31–32).

The Banner Lifted High

He was indeed the banner that was lifted up most fully on the cross. There is where the battle for our souls was fully engaged—and there is also where it was won—"It is finished!" was His victorious cry. Look to Christ and find life. For Christ was not confined to death, but He burst through the gates of hell to proclaim His victory, and at the appointed hour the stone of His tomb was removed.

His banner is held high this day, whether we remember the coming of our Lord as a child or as we ponder the depths of His sacrificial death on the cross. Whether we engage in worship or in the battles of our life, we go forward in the assurance of God's love for us and His undying devotion to gather us, as His holy people. The One who established for us the covenant of His love did so with the shedding of His own blood. Jesus remains lifted high among us. He is praised for the grace delivered to us in His Word, bestowed in and through Baptism and in the sustenance of His body and blood in Holy Communion. He is lifted high that all may know that salvation comes from the Lord—His banner is for all to see; it is a banner that draws people from all nations to the victor's side.

For the proclamation has been made by our Lord, and it moves across the face of this earth and certainly through your life and home: Your Savior has come! He has been lifted high! The banner over you is God's majestic love in Jesus Christ.

Rev. Eric L. Zacharias

Epiphany

Epiphany

THE TRUE LIGHT SHINES
Isaiah 60:1

Light is so important, be it physical—created already on the first day—or spiritual. We cannot live without it. No one wants to be benighted. We prefer to be enlightened.

Years ago, from the time called the Enlightenment, the German philosopher Gottfried Wilhelm Leibniz grandly judged his era: "This is the best of all possible worlds." The French wit Voltaire penned his satire *Candide* to lampoon the optimism Leibniz's line engendered in some, yet even Voltaire could not resist and hailed this new Age of Reason as the greatest epoch the world had known. Things weren't finished, and no one claimed to be completely enlightened, but the process was underway; life was becoming clear in this Age of Enlightenment. Victory is just a matter of time. And why not? Superstitions were falling by the wayside, and unfettered, natural human reason would triumph. As Alexander Pope observed: "Nature and nature's laws lay hid in night. God said, 'Let Newton be!' And all was light."

But the Age of Reason gave way not to utopia but to revolution and bloodletting. Spurning their melioristic optimism and given a more realistic anthropology, we hardly ought to be surprised. Yet even as a new round of darkness closed in and the temporary light faded, people refused to see the light, so to speak. They sought new sources of illumination. It's all too human, this side of Genesis 3. Each day's sunrise and sunset with the dark that follows is a kind of metaphor for how history goes "under the sun" (Eccl 1:3)—life in the squirrel cage. We get busy in the day and "make hay while the sun shines," but night always follows. What can we get done, groping in the dark when we can't see?

In the physical world we won't take "no" for an answer, so we seek to turn night to day. Cities blaze and some never seem to sleep. Intellectually and especially spiritually, we also fight to hold off the dark. On his deathbed, Goethe is said to have cried out, "More light!" Beyond flinging open the shutters—what Goethe apparently wanted—we can't help but wonder about fear of a spiritual curtain being drawn, a darkness closing in at life's end as light fades.

Where to find the answer? Where do we find light for life? Ironically, true light comes shining through when all seems dark. Truth appears, not beneath a blinding sun, but in midnight skies with barely a glimmer. To be precise, three skies catch our attention for the moment.

First, centuries ago, God took Abram out under the night sky and gave him a promise: new land, descendants numbered like those countless stars, and news that through him and his offspring all nations would be blessed. In the dark, Abram saw the light. Stars hung above as a sign. He believed and it was counted to him as righteousness.

Centuries later his offspring were held captive in foreign darkness. But though the night sky looks a bit different in Babylon, stars remained; God was not through fulfilling that earlier promise. And if Abraham's descendants wanted to hear more, they could listen to the words of the prophet Isaiah (60:1): "Arise, shine, for your light has come." The Messiah and deliverance still stand large in God's plan. He will not let the darkness triumph. Light for their spiritual life is theirs. God's glory shines in deliverance. They may not yet see its fulfillment, in their return and in the Messiah, but like light from the stars, it is already fact, already on the way, for God has spoken it.

On to yet a third look generations later, where in another nighttime sky the stars shone again and the light appeared, this time in a special star seen in the East. Whether the Wise Men realized it or not, the promise to Abraham had been fulfilled—that all nations were now blessed, that the glory of the Lord had indeed broken forth. The promise was made flesh, and light broke into darkness. Light shined forth life. Where is this glory? Where God's love is manifest, where sinners are saved. It was all in a child. Were it not for God's grace, and for the faith He gives, no one would have seen that light.

And what of us? "Wise men seek Him still," the saying goes. True enough. But seek Him where? In the stars? Stargazing in the city is wasted effort, we know, for the artificial glow from city lights clouds the view. Perhaps we can take that, too, as a metaphor for how so much spiritual searching goes today. Glaring street lamps, headlight ribbons on the freeways, dazzling marquees, and flashing neon all compete for attention: Look here! Look at me! The stars that once stood as a sign are all but lost amid the pollution. Attention is diverted to the glitzy, seduced by artificial lights. It's no accident that Satan deceives as Lucifer, bearer of light.

But God leaves nothing to chance. We are not off on our own. He makes sure we see His light by inviting us to look in the right place. The heavens aren't our focus. Abraham's promise is fulfilled. The Epiphany star has come and gone. But the glory of the Lord is still risen and shines on us, seen not where we might think to look, but where God directs our sight. So the spotlight falls not on a throne room but on the manger with the infant Redeemer. Then on to the focal point of Christ's coming: in the midst of Good Friday's midday darkness we see death, but God sends forth spiritual light. Who would think a cross could shine like His?

The Easter dawn that beams into the empty tomb confirms it all. And to make sure we know that this is ours, so we can't miss His saving love, He blocks our way and focuses His light with laser precision right in front of our eyes. The things illuminated may seem unlikely, but they are His gifts with His promises to us: Baptism; word of forgiveness declared; Word fixed to bread and wine—Christ given for us for forgiveness of sin. Here is God's glory risen to shine on us in salvation. Here is light from above; light to end all darkness; light from no sun, moon, or stars, but light in and from Christ, the light of the world for all eternity.

This side of the parousia, Leibniz was right after all (though hardly as he thought). This is the best of all possible worlds. The Sun of Righteousness is risen; Epiphany has dawned; the light shines and we bask in its glow.

Rev. Robert L. Rosin

Desires Made Manifest

Matthew 2:1–12

Some people living in a major metropolitan city were asked in a survey what was the most annoying part of their workday. A large percentage said the morning commute to work was the most frustrating and annoying. When asked what made it so annoying, the responses varied. "There is no limit to the number of people and the number of times you see people doing stupid things." "Other than the slowness of the traffic, you have to deal with people cutting from the slower lane to the faster lane and then back to the other when it seems to go faster."

If you've ever driven in a metro area you can relate to these observations. Can you imagine how much faster traffic would be if everyone got in the lane they needed and stayed there? We often wonder why people want or desire to cut back and forth from lane to lane. And if you think about it, it's really quite simple—they want or desire to get into the faster lane. Yet at best, this is just a surface want or desire.

The desire for a faster lane is driven by a deeper, what I would call a secondary, desire. This secondary desire isn't hard to figure out. They want to get to work on time. But this deeper or secondary desire is not the real reason they drive so crazy. Behind this is the primary desire of keeping their job. The desire to keep the job gave rise to the desire to get to work on time, which then gave rise to their desire to jump from lane to lane in search of the fastest lane in traffic.

In our text we find desires driving the events. We have the desire of the Magi, of Herod, and of God.

THE MAGI

The surface desire of the Magi was to find the one born King of the Jews. Behind the surface desire was the secondary desire. Our text tells us their secondary desire: "We . . . have come to worship Him" (Mt 2:2b)

Once they found the child, they revealed their primary desire. "Opening their treasures, they offered Him gifts, gold and frankincense and myrrh" (2:11b). All their desires were driven by a desire to give gifts to the newborn King, which demonstrated His worth to them.

HEROD

Herod also desired to find the Christ. The surface desire is revealed when he asks the chief priests and teachers of the law where the Christ was to be born. It is further verified by his command to the Magi to make a careful search for the Christ Child and then come and tell him what they have discovered. At this point, the surface desires of Herod and the Magi are the same.

But Herod had a secondary desire. He said that he, too, wanted to worship the new King. But when Herod learned of the Christ Child's birth, he became troubled—and all Jerusalem was equally troubled. Jerusalem was troubled because the last time Herod thought someone was trying to take his throne, he killed his two sons and all associated with them. Some years later Herod killed his wife and all those associated with her.

Herod's secondary desire was to kill the Christ Child. Herod's primary desire was to remain king. To satisfy his desire to remain king and keep his kingdom, Herod had to kill the real, the rightful King. Herod desired to keep a kingdom that was, in truth, not his.

GOD

This desire—to keep or to be what one is not—not only affects kings like Herod but is common to one and all. It began with Adam and Eve, as they desired to be what they were not—like God. Since that day, since that first sinful desire, we have all been plagued and held captive by the same selfish, self-serving, primary desire.

Consider some surface desires in our daily life. How often do you desire to tell a lie? The primary desire is still to keep or to be what one is not—to escape the consequences of our actions or to get something we cannot get with the truth. To satisfy this primary desire, we tell a lie. The only way we can do this is to get rid of Jesus—get rid of the truth. It is here that we come face-to-face with the desire of Herod and the desire of God.

We have just celebrated the birth of the Christ Child. God desired that His Son come to our world and take on our flesh and live among us. Yet this is actually a surface desire. While this is one of God's desires, it is not His primary desire. God's primary desire is to seek and to save that which is lost; that is, to save you and me from the consequences of our sinful actions and our sinfulness from birth. To satisfy this desire, God sent Jesus to take on flesh, to live among us, and to go the way of the cross.

God laid all our sinfulness, all the times we have gotten rid of Jesus, or sought to get rid of Him, on Jesus as He was crucified. For all the times we jump from one self-serving lane of life to another, Jesus was gotten rid of in death.

God loved His only-begotten Son, but He also knew that the only way to get rid of the barrier of sin, the barrier of death between Him and us, was to have His Son take these things away in His own death on the cross. The resurrection of Jesus is the joyous assurance that through His suffering and death, Jesus satisfied God the Father's primary desire. For on His cross Jesus met you, met me, and met our world where we are. We were lost among the self-serving desires that drive us farther and farther from the Lord. Having met us, Jesus saves us.

At Epiphany we celebrate the manifestation or revelation of Jesus as Savior of the world. One of the major elements of our Christmas observations is the star. In the sending of the star, God's desires are seen again. Apart from the Jewish people, who would know that a Savior was born? God desired that all the world, both Jews and non-Jews, know the Savior had come. God's primary desire in revealing this infant King was that all might believe in Him.

In our Baptism God's primary desire was satisfied as the Savior is born in us. The light we follow is Jesus Christ.

In the new life of Baptism our desires become those of the Magi, seeking Jesus and finding Jesus, not in a manger but in His Word, in worship, in the Supper He serves us with His own body and blood. Having found Him we might worship Him, receive of His presence, and open to Him our treasures of praise and thanksgiving, of service and sharing the Good News of Him who has found us and saved us.

We live in a world that tends to manifest its primary desires in emotionally and physically violent and cruel self-serving ways. Epiphany reminds us of our God, who has revealed that His primary desire was to manifest His great love and saving presence to us all. Jesus declared, and this is our Epiphany confidence, "I came that they may have life and have it abundantly" (Jn 10:10).

Rev. Mark W. Love